Dedicated to Linda Eisele

October, 2008

ISBN 978-0-615-25848-5

Please forward any questions or comments regarding this manual to info@attach.org.

Contents

CHAPTER 1

Introduction

This manual is designed to help parents of children who have disorders of attachment learn to parent their children effectively. By "effectively" we mean in a manner that:

- helps children to heal from the trauma or maltreatment they experienced early in life from relationships with primary caregivers
- helps children form secure attachments with their current primary caregiver, providing the foundation of trust that is necessary for successful relationships in all aspects of their lives
- helps the children learn the skills they need to be successful in life

This manual assumes that the child has been diagnosed by a qualified attachment therapist as having a disorder of attachment, and that organic barriers to attachment have been ruled out through a complete medical exam (including hearing, vision, sensory integration testing and assessment for other developmental problems). If this is not the case, see attach.org for a referral to a local therapist who specializes in diagnosing and treating disorders of attachment.

This manual also assumes that you have a basic understanding of disorders of attachment, their underlying causes, and their symptoms (see attach.org for more information). It is not intended to replace the guidance of a qualified attachment therapist, but rather to supplement therapy by painting a clear picture of the current professional thinking about treating disorders of attachment and how to apply those philosophies to real-life parenting challenges.

Because of their unresolved relationship trauma, children often react to current, nurturing caregivers with the same defensive behaviors they needed to survive their early trauma. This is a difficult concept to keep in mind, when, for example, you take your child to the latest movie that he is anxious to see, buy tickets, popcorn and sodas and get settled into your seat in time to watch the previews, but five minutes into the movie he starts screaming that he wants to go home! How embarrassing! And infuriating! Is he being a difficult child who just changed his mind and expects to get his way? Is he just trying to punish you for making him go to bed early last night? Or is it that he is so distrustful of adults, due to his early abuse, that it is truly terrifying for him to sit next to anyone for more than 15 minutes? How you diagnose the behavior, and respond to it, will determine whether or not you help your child, and your relationship, to move forward.

Parenting a child who has a disorder of attachment is the hardest job you will ever have. Period. It requires you to give and give, without receiving much in return (at least in the beginning). It requires rethinking your parenting instincts, experience with other children, and advice on child rearing. It means making conscious, therapeutic parenting decisions, hour after hour, day after day, week after week. It requires constant focus on the deeper meaning of your child's behavior, so that you respond to the causes, needs, and motivations of your child. It is exhausting. It is isolating, as family and friends tend to keep their distance, uncomfortable with the drama that surrounds these children. After all that, inevitably some teacher, coach, or therapist who does not understand attachment issues will tell you that it's *you* who is the problem. In actuality, the issue is how your child's hurts from the past make connection with a caregiver in the present so hard.

So why do it? It's simple. To give your child a second chance to have a good life. Regardless of the outcome, what a wonderful gift! But providing "a good home" is not enough. To do the job well, you need to truly understand your child's issues, so that you can create a therapeutic home environment that helps your child heal, as well as seek the additional resources he or she may need. It is ATTACh's hope that this manual will truly help.

The information contained in this manual was compiled by the following committee of ATTACh members and board of directors, all of whom specialize in treating disorders of attachment and many of whom are also parents of children who have disorders of attachment:

Connie Hornyak, LCSW, Chair

JoAnn Vesper, LICSW, Co-chair

Arthur Becker-Weidman, PhD

Marilyn Durbin, LCSW

Mary Lou Edgar, LCSW

Janice Goldwater, LCSW

Bernadine Janzen, MS, LPC

Victoria Kelly, LCSW, Psy.D., MHA

Keith Kuboyama, LCSW

Jacqueline Rushing, LCSW

Lynn Wetterberg, MS

*Contribution and editing by Kelly Frey, former board member, parent advocate.

CHAPTER 2

The Attachment Puzzle: How Our Histories Fit Together

Raising and trying to heal a child with a disorder of attachment or serious attachment disturbance is clearly a daunting challenge. Typically, parents struggle alone with the overwhelming sense that something is terribly wrong, but not knowing what it is or how to fix it. Often, children with serious attachment problems manage to divide the adults in their lives, pitting the outside world against the family. This is usually a defensive strategy that helps them prevent closeness with their parents—the thing that they most fear! Sadly, this is often misunderstood by the outside world and the parents are blamed for the problems. Without a way to understand what is happening, it is too easy for parents to then blame themselves. And sometimes, when parents are at the end of their ropes, it is too easy to blame the child. At a time when a vulnerable family most needs help, support, and understanding, too often the result is to become more isolated and estranged from supportive resources.

Parents are then left alone in their own struggles to try to reach, manage, and help their clearly wounded child. For many parents, when they first learn of the terms "attachment disorder" or "Reactive Attachment Disorder", it is literally like someone threw them a life line when they were drowning in a storm at sea. Suddenly, there is a name for this problem that has overwhelmed their family, robbed them of even basic connection with their child, and, perhaps, even caused them to profoundly doubt their ability to be a parent. Sadly, for many, this momentary sense of hope is often then shattered by stories of devastating outcomes for these children. The purpose of this handbook is try to help parents understand this very serious challenge to their children's development and functioning, while offering practical help.

Parent attachment issues—an important piece of the puzzle

Part of understanding how to be truly helpful to your child in his or her journey toward healing is to understand what a disorder of attachment or attachment disturbance actually is. Additionally, thinking about our own attachment histories can help us appreciate how hard it can be to change these deeply ingrained ways of relating. Bearing witness to these children's emotional wounds, and extending ourselves to help them heal, can pull on both the parent's and therapist's own attachment experiences. Adults may have learned how to function well in the world without having fully resolved hurts they experienced as children in their own families. They may have decided that there is no point in rehashing what is in the past. They may have gotten to a point where they understand things with their heads, while hiding the hurts that persist in their hearts. Coping this way might have worked well until the parents are faced with trying to help their wounded children heal. Suddenly, these well-functioning parents can find that what has worked for them in the past no longer works. Long-buried feelings of hurt or self-doubts may start to emerge. The parents may find themselves responding with anger, sometimes in ways that feel inappropriate or excessive. Sometimes the parents may put on blinders to avoid facing their children's painful histories. If they have learned to cope by just "letting bygones be bygones," they may be shocked at how easily triggered and reactive their children can be. All of these very normal feelings can make parents feel worse and worse about themselves or angrier and angrier with the child. But there is reason for hope! Research has clearly shown us that, as those parents find ways to heal their own unresolved attachment wounds, they can be much more effective parents for a wounded, challenging child.

To understand how attachment affects the development of the person from childhood to adulthood, we need to start by distinguishing normal attachment styles from real disturbances in attachment that can become disorders of attachment. **Attachment is not something that exists in the child alone; rather, it is how that child learns to connect with and relate to significant others—especially parents and primary caregivers**. Effective attachment-focused therapy therefore needs to center on the relationship you have with your child. Some parents are confused by this since the problem behaviors clearly exist in the child. If parents are asked to participate in their children's therapy, or if a therapist recommends that they also do some therapy for themselves, they fear being blamed for their child's problems. Unfortunately, some therapists who do not understand attachment problems might do that, since therapists are often taught to think of the child's problems as part of the larger "family system." However, good attachment-focused therapy recognizes that family systems change—while the child has had other family experiences that have shaped him, his family is now different, whether a new adoptive family or a recovered birth family. The child may be able to learn that things have really changed.

Yet, the past shapes us all. Often times past relationships have given us one "road map" about how to relate to others that is based (to differing degrees) on feelings of fear, mistrust, and avoidance. New and healthier relationships can help us develop "road maps" that lead to connection, trust, and healthy relationships. However, giving up the old familiar maps is not easy. Indeed, it can be very challenging. When we have traveled the same roads to the same destinations so often, we no longer even think we are following a map—we are just living in the only reality we know.

What is important to remember is that the child's behaviors are symptoms of distorted thinking and feeling that came from early experiences with primary caregivers. We cannot talk children out of these ways of being. We cannot punish children out of these ways of being (indeed, doing so may only make it worse!). Instead, we need to help children *experience* their way out of these habits of relating by offering them healthy relationships that provide the kinds of nurturing experiences they needed when they were younger. The kind of experience they most need is experience with new or recovered parents who can really feel what it is to be them; help them make sense of what has happened to them in a way that does not mean they are unlovable and unworthy; and, learn new ways of relating that allow emotional connection and trust to grow. That can be a challenge when the child actively pushes against the parent's attempts to love and care for the child.

Forming secure attachments

A child's way of attaching to others is not something the child chooses, nor can he change it by trying without external help. It is the result of the child's experiences with early caregiving. Children who had the good fortune to experience "good enough" caregiving received nurturance, security, comfort, encouragement, and positive recognition. Fortunately, children do not require perfect parents, since there are none! Instead, the term "good enough" is used to suggest that, on the whole, the balance has clearly been in favor of meeting the child's needs in a way that was responsive to the particular child. This takes into account that there is also some important value in children learning to handle situations when their needs are not met immediately. In these situations, the "good enough" parent recognizes the child's distress and helps comfort the child, teaches the child to tolerate and handle negative feelings, and repairs the sense of a break in the relationship. The concept of "good enough" parenting also takes into account the reality that children are all different. An easygoing, flexible child may be able to handle less attention or active support than a fussy, easily overwhelmed child would need.

Children whose needs were well met by their primary caregiver have a better chance of developing what is called "secure attachment." Secure attachment is shown by a child who is comfortable with physical and emotional closeness, is able to share a variety of emotions, and usually seems confident in exploring new things. These children have learned through experience that other people are basically good, helpful, and trustworthy. Moreover, when other people respond to them in that way, these children experience themselves as good, lovable, valuable, and competent. The world is therefore seen as a mostly safe and predictable place. There is comfort and help available when the inevitable bumps in the road happen, so children learn a sense of trust and resiliency. They learn to trust that their primary caregiver is a "secure base," or a source of comfort and help when the challenges of life inevitably face them.

How insecure attachments form

Unfortunately, only about 60 - 65 percent of all of us had the kind of beginning in life that fosters secure attachments. Across the general public, some 35 – 40 percent of individuals develop what is referred to as "insecure attachment." These individuals' early experience did not help them develop that real sense of security in others or the world. Their early experiences did not teach them that they were unconditionally lovable; rather, they learned that there were limits and conditions to their receiving love, approval and/or acceptance. They were left with doubts about themselves—doubts about whether they were really lovable, valuable, and competent. Among groups with higher risks for vulnerability (for example, families involved in the child welfare system), even a greater number of their children might experience insecure attachments.

However, insecure attachment styles are not pathological. They are not clinical diagnoses, although it is likely that more children with insecure attachment styles than children with secure attachment styles will have psychological problems. They are normal responses to experiences in which parents are, to differing degrees, unable to provide sensitive, empathic responses to the child's needs or flexibly respond to the child's needs instead of imposing the parent's needs. They represent normal coping responses to the situations in which very likely the parent's good intentions were overwhelmed or compromised by other demands, crises, or life challenges. Such situations might have involved circumstances such as a parent's depression, unresolved grief, domestic violence, substance abuse, mental illness, lengthy absence, or child abuse. As you might imagine, some of these situations could lead to relatively minor caregiving lapses, while others, or more serious forms of any of them, might lead to the child being neglected or seriously hurt.

Young children are extremely dependent on their caregivers, and therefore need to be able to stay in the relationship with the caregiver. The attachment style the child develops becomes a sort of road map for how to stay in the relationship, like a dance between the child and caregiver. At first, the caregiver must fit her dancing to lead the very young child. But as the child grows, he may learn that he will only be able to keep the dance going if he accommodates to the limits of his caregiver's ability to give him what he needs. He may need to act as if he doesn't really need as much as he really does, so as not to overwhelm her with his needs. Or he may intensify his expression of need, with the hope that he won't be forgotten and might instead then get some minimum needs met. In more mild degrees these experiences may create insecure attachment styles, while in more extreme cases they may create disorders of attachment.

Avoidant attachment style

For children who develop an insecure attachment style, their attachment experiences typically included differing degrees of inadequate experiences of security, comfort, and assistance. Some develop what is referred to as an "avoidant" attachment style. On the surface, these children might first appear to be very independent and emotionally self-reliant. However, this is more of a defensive response; they have accommodated by learning that their caregiver will meet their needs best if they don't seem to need much. These children learn to depend less on their caregiver as a secure base for comfort, solace, or help. They tend to show less emotional expression in general, and in particular seem to cut off and disguise their feelings of anger or hurt with a sense of indifference. Again, experience has taught these children to adapt their responses to the caregiver. These responses make sense when the caregiver rejects the child's needs to some degree. These responses make sense when the caregiver is uncomfortable with emotional and/or physical closeness and intimacy. These responses make sense when the caregiver seems unable to fully recognize and share in the child's feelings. These responses also make sense when the caregiver communicates that he/she cannot handle the child's needs and must push the child away either physically or emotionally. These responses can lead children to be overly self-reliant, uncomfortable with intense feelings (their own or those of others), and less able to recognize their own needs. They may cope by trying to stay busy so as to avoid difficult feelings of frustration and loneliness.

Ambivalent attachment style

Others with feelings of insecurity may develop what is referred to as an "ambivalent" attachment style. These children are also hurt and angry, but have not crossed over into a protective stance of defensive indifference like those who have an avoidant style. Instead, their strong longing for connection and comfort is often spoiled with feelings of anger and frustration. They seem desperately focused on trying to gain their parent's attention and assure the parent's availability. They lack trust that the parent will be there as a true "secure base" when needed. This results in a tendency toward an anxious conflict between wanting to explore the world, yet fretting that there will be no "safe harbor" to return to when most needed. They may show a confused response of clinging, attempts to push away, and frustration at never being really satisfied either way. This can also result in a tendency to hold back from trying new experiences or risking new adventures. Many of these children learn that the way to increase the likelihood of receiving the caregiver's attention is to turn up the volume of their feelings and demands or to exaggerate their helplessness. These responses make sense if the child's experience is that the caregiver is inconsistent in his/her availability and attention. These responses make sense if the child has learned that if he complains loudly or bitterly enough, the caregiver will respond. This can lead to a preoccupation with the caregiver in a desperate desire to hold on to and even control the caregiver. These responses can lead to individuals who doubt their ability to get their needs met in healthy ways. Instead, these individuals may struggle with developing and maintaining healthy boundaries with others and therefore may be vulnerable to becoming involved with others in unhealthy ways. They may try to cope with life by staying preoccupied with how their relationships are working, so that they spend significant energy in worrying about maintaining connections. They may fret over minor disagreements and need to seek repeated reassurance that things are okay.

Disorganized attachment style

Others with feelings of insecurity may develop what is referred to as a "disorganized" attachment style. In this style, the child's insecurity is less about frustration and unmet longing for connection and more about actual fearfulness. These children tend to respond in contradictory and even at times bizarre ways toward their caregivers. They show fear and confusion. Sometimes they seem frozen and unable to respond. At other times they may show very contradictory "push-pull" reactions—that is, they may feel the need to move toward their caregiver for closeness only to then react with an equally strong need to push away. These responses make sense when the caregiver, who has been the child's source of security, also becomes the source of the child's fear. The child is faced with an impossible bind: the natural instinct for young children to seek closeness and comfort to survive conflicts with the child's sense that the caregiver is unsafe and perhaps even frightening. The overwhelming contradiction is so confusing and frightening that the child is unable to learn how to navigate the relationship with the parent. Instead, the child is so fearful that the defensive responses of fight, flight or freeze become the natural reactions to the caregiver. These responses are more common when the caregiver has been the source of the child's abuse, the child is exposed to serious domestic violence, or when the caregiver has serious mental health and/or substance abuse problems. The child is then also left alone with his or her terror and is afraid to seek the caregiver for support and help in getting calm or feeling safe. These children are left with unresolved traumatic memories that can become "triggers" for defensive reactions in which they later fight, flee, or freeze in situations where that kind of response is not necessary. For example, a mild verbal scolding years later may trigger the child's feelings from the earlier abuse. The child may run away from or attack the person doing the scolding, or may freeze, unable to even mutter a reply. Children who have had this kind of early experience with attachment figures, and who do not get help resolving the trauma, may become very fearful of connection with others and easily overwhelmed and confused by their own feelings. Children with disorganized attachment relationships are much more likely than those with any of the other attachment styles to develop serious emotional and behavioral problems, including disorders of attachment.

Old roadmaps in a new relationship

All of these insecure attachment patterns are ways of relating to specific important people in the person's life. These patterns become like "road maps" about how to relate with others. They tell us what to expect of others and how to respond to others' behavior. When an old road map is used to navigate new relationships, it can lead us to develop the same familiar kinds of relationships. The reason is that these road maps are so much a part of who we are and how we perceive the world that we forget they are just maps, not the whole picture. For instance, if we have not learned to trust the good will of our caregivers toward us when we were young, we will expect that new people will also not be trustworthy. Fortunately, it is possible to create different maps to teach us new ways to navigate relationships. This is possible when a new person refuses to drive with us on our old map, but instead helps us understand that we can together explore and enjoy the creation of a new map. It only takes one such experience to start to change us, if that relationship can provide more in the way of acceptance for who we are and can recognize our needs, feelings, and hopes. That kind of relationship can be the bridge to a different future. It can be both the bridge to a deeper sense of connection with someone else and with our own self. When we "feel felt by" another, we can learn to recognize our own feelings and needs, and begin to see our own struggles from a new perspective. This bridge helps us cross from a past of insecurity in attachment to what is called "acquired" or "achieved" security. This does not mean that the past is forgotten or that it cannot, from time to time, "hijack" us back to some earlier emotional reaction. Instead, it means that we are better able to live more fully in the present. We can better accept both the good times and the hard times as valuable parts of what makes us who we are. We are better able to realize that we are greater than the sum of all these experiences and no longer defined by any one of them. We find new ways to understand our past and link it to a more positive future.

For those adults who have reached "acquired" or "achieved" security, there can be a real benefit in increased capacity for empathy and compassion for others still on the journey. Many parents who come to adoption do so from a need to transform their own history of loss by helping make a child's life whole. Some parents who have found their way on their own path to recovery from substance abuse, depression, other mental illness, or domestic violence, have also found or reclaimed a sense of security and self-esteem that now makes it possible to understand and provide compassionate help to their wounded children.

When considering the information presented in this chapter thus far, parents might notice a mixture of feelings. They might feel hopeful that their own experiences of achieving greater security in attachment could be useful in helping their children heal. Yet, that feeling of optimism might soon give way to confusion or discouragement if their own child is not making progress toward healing in spite of good care. They may also feel discouraged if they, from time to time, feel "triggered" back into patterns more like the old ones from which they thought they had broken free. These reactions take us back to the question of what disorders of attachment really are. What has been described so far are "styles" of attachment that are found across the general public.

In normal development, a child might have one kind of attachment pattern with one parent and a different kind with the other parent. For example, a child might have a secure pattern with her mother and an avoidant pattern with her father or vice versa. Or, a child might have an ambivalent pattern with his mother and an avoidant pattern with his father and so on. The pattern is specific to the particular relationship. In such patterns, a child will still bring that "road map" into new relationships, but the child will be able to learn that new relationships can be different and new maps are needed. Over time, with new experience, the child might well learn that different expectations and rules govern the new relationship. The child then may develop a different attachment pattern than she or he has known before. The child with an avoidant pattern may become more comfortable with emotional closeness and able to admit his need for help. The child with an ambivalent style may become more trusting in others so that she is less anxious when they are not immediately available. The child with a disorganized style may become less fearful and begin to develop greater trust in the caregiver.

Disorders of attachment

We also know that some children (and some adults) persist in their attachment style no matter what new relationship they encounter or how old relationships change. In these cases, we begin to recognize that the child's way of reacting toward others is not responsive to the present relationship with someone else; instead, the child's reactions seem more fixed or even stuck in the predictable patterns that served him in past relationships. The child's perceptions and beliefs remain rigidly fixed so that new experience and information cannot change them. It is very concerning when the child's pattern of reactions seems stuck, so that no matter how much new and different experience the child gets with a nurturing and sensitive caregiver (or caregivers) the same reactions continue. This is most troubling when the child continues to react with defensive responses to offers of supportive and nurturing care. In these situations we begin to suspect that instead of an attachment "style," the child has a "disorder" of attachment. **Disorders are defined as chronic patterns of behavior that are not constructive, that cause problems for the child's functioning in the present, and that may cause delays or even distortions in the child's development.**

Children with disturbances and even disorders in their attachment require strong, healthy, committed relationships in which to heal. Yet, they can present significant challenges for anyone attempting to be in relationship with them and to help them. Their experiences of hurt, rejection, betrayal, coercion, and exploitation have taught them well not to trust or rely on others. With these hurtful treatments, they have experienced themselves as bad, unlovable, unworthy, and somehow at fault. They have learned that being loved also means being hurt. These experiences have also taught them that the world is a dangerous and unpredictable place. In order to survive, they have needed to learn good defenses—to push others away; to resist showing their needs and vulnerabilities; and, perhaps, even to hurt others before they can be hurt.

The defensive behaviors of these children can be very hurtful to their parents. No matter how much the parents understand about why the child reacts this way, the knowledge is not enough to prevent the parents from at least sometimes taking the hurtful behaviors and words personally. If the parents' hurt then causes them to turn away from the child or respond in anger, this can be interpreted by the child as proof that the parents are no different than those earlier caregivers who let him down or hurt him. While it is easy to say that parents should not take things personally, it is very hard to do that in the heat of the moment, in the face of such powerful experiences of hurt and rejection. Yet, we know that it can become easier if parents have a way of understanding their own attachment-related triggers and issues.

Understanding adult attachment patterns

This leads us back to understanding our own attachment styles as adults. Attachment styles may not be as easy to see in adults as in young children, but they are there all the same. They may be most easy to see when we are under stress or feel threatened (certainly parenting a child with a disorder of attachment may often present a powerful perceived threat to the parents' sense of self-esteem and even competency.) Our attachment styles are the legacy we carry from own experiences as children. Most parents have had the experience of doing or saying something that is "just like their parents," even if they had sworn to themselves they would be different. The very experience of being a parent, with all its powerful emotions, pulls on us in many ways. It can reawaken old longings, revive old hurts and rekindle old fears. Usually, these experiences help motivate us to do it differently for our children. But in spite of our best efforts and intentions, sometimes it can be very difficult to shield our children from our own hurts and fears. Parents consume parenting books in an effort to do it right for their children. But these books tend to focus on techniques. **They rarely provide help for us in looking inside ourselves so that we can better understand our own motivations, conflicts, unmet needs, and fears.** In fact, it usually takes another person's gentle challenge to help us learn to look at these vulnerable parts of ourselves more honestly. Unless we can do that, these can have power over us that interfere with our intentions and efforts to be sensitive, emotionally present parents.

We need to be able to bear witness to our children's pain and hurts. This is hard enough for any parent, but it is much harder for parents whose own painful memories and unresolved feelings are revived when they begin to really feel for their child. The coping strategies of these parents, constructed long ago to keep them from being overwhelmed by their feelings, may be real barriers to being consistently present in the sensitive, responsive way that wounded children need to heal. It is important to stress that this is ***not*** to blame parents. Adoptive parents did not cause their children's pain. Birth parents, whose actions or inactions did cause their children pain, invariably wanted something better for their children. Regardless of what happened to cause the child's pain and wounds, the parents in the present have the obligation to do things differently so that the child can heal. **To be able to do things differently in the present, parents need to be able to understand how the legacy of their own childhood experiences may affect their children in the present.** That legacy is present in the parents' own attachment style.

Secure-autonomous attachment style

In adults, the secure attachment style is called “secure-autonomous” attachment. These people are comfortable both with closeness and with autonomy. They are generally comfortable with feelings, and comfortable depending on others and having others depend on them. They are not overly fearful of abandonment or being smothered. It is important to recognize that some of these adults did in fact have unhappy and difficult childhoods. However, they have been able, for the most part, to make peace with their past. They can acknowledge both the good and the difficult times, and realistically see the strengths and areas of weakness in their parents. They can honestly tell the stories of their lives with a range of emotions and with a perspective that honors all of the journey.

Parents who have secure attachment patterns have a greater chance of helping their children achieve security in attachment. However, even parents with a Secure-autonomous attachment can be overwhelmed by a child with a disorder of attachment. Yet, these parents will be more likely to recognize and accept his or her feelings, to ask for help, and to find supports to cope with the struggles.

Insecure attachment styles

In adults there are also insecure patterns of attachment.

Dismissing attachment style

The pattern most like the avoidant pattern in children is called the “dismissing style” in adults. This label can be a bit confusing. These individuals can be very loving toward and interested in others—it is not necessarily that they dismiss others from their lives. Instead, what they do guard against is looking inward at their own feelings or memories. They tend to “dismiss” those as not that important and as best left “in the past”. They might idealize their parents, but speak of them in vague or overly general ways. Sometimes they may acknowledge that they confronted difficult things in the past, but may try to quickly brush away the impact of the past with statements such as "it made me a stronger person." The difference between this pattern and the autonomous pattern, is that these people lack a real sense of connection with the feelings associated with the past experience. Instead, they may ignore or make little of those feelings. They may take on a "stiff upper lip" approach of minimizing the impact of hard experiences. This is likely a defensive reaction to try to ward off painful feelings of hurt or rejection. They tend to be very self reliant individuals who are better at taking care of others than of themselves. They find it difficult to truly rely on others. They may use activity as a way to avoid difficult feelings. Parents with a dismissing style of attachment are more likely to have children with avoidant patterns of attachment, unless they can achieve greater security for themselves.

Parents with dismissing styles will likely have special challenges in parenting a child with an attachment disorder. These parents may find themselves avoiding the child's strong negative feelings by either failing to recognize them or hurrying to smooth things over when the feelings emerge. These parents may be vulnerable to becoming preoccupied with the tasks of parenting, seeking treatment resources, or researching information, striving to appear committed to the child's healing. However, underneath this activity is a need to distance themselves from their child's emotional distress. Some of these parents may resist any exploration of the child's traumatic memories with a conviction of "not stirring things up" or retraumatizing the child, when much of the resistance is actually the parents' own fears of confronting such distressing feelings. Some of these parents may overwork or spread themselves too thin in an effort to take care of others, while ignoring their own needs. They may minimize the hurt they feel from their child's rejection, which can unintentionally undermine important messages to the child about just how much the relationship really means to them. They are often reluctant to let others know what they need or how overwhelmed they truly feel. This can lead to isolation and estrangement, which can intensify the feelings of desperation. Parents with a dismissing attachment style have a greater chance of having children with an avoidant style, unless the parent can reach greater levels of security themselves.

Preoccupied attachment style

The pattern most like the ambivalent style in children is called the "preoccupied" style in adults. These individuals can speak about past hurts and disappointments, often with an intensity that makes it feel as if those were recent wounds, when they might instead be decades old. These individuals tell the stories of their lives as filled with unsuccessful attempts to please their parents along with the resulting frustration and disappointment born of those experiences. Often, these individuals can become so caught up in the emotions of relationships that they fail to see their own role in conflicts. This can lead to ongoing frustration with an inability to get as close to others as they would like. This can also lead to a vulnerability to feeling easily hurt and estranged from others, even during normal conflicts that arise in daily living.

Parents with a preoccupied attachment style may also have special challenges when parenting a child with a disorder of attachment. When the child reacts in defensive ways to push the parents away, these parents may have a particularly hard time not personalizing that. This rejection may echo against the past feelings of rejection and erode the parents' sense of self-esteem. These parents may have learned as children to intensify the expression of feelings to enlist help. This approach may backfire with the child who has a disorder of attachment. Instead of the parents helping the child regain emotional balance, the parents may inadvertently escalate the emotional expressions. The child may feel that the parents are too fearful or weak to really handle the child's intense anger and/or fear. These parents, in an effort to keep the peace at all costs, may placate the child and not be able to set appropriate limits. Sometimes, as the family conflict and chaos escalates, these parents may desperately seek help, but unconsciously need to keep the focus on the latest crisis as a way of protecting their fear of their own inadequacy as a parent. Parents with a preoccupied attachment style have a greater chance of having children with an ambivalent style unless the parents can reach greater levels of security themselves.

Unresolved, fearful attachment style

The pattern most like the disorganized pattern in children is the "unresolved, fearful" pattern in adults. These are the parents whose own unresolved histories of trauma and loss continue to compromise their functioning in the present. These are the parents who are most at risk of becoming overwhelmed by their children's own unresolved traumatic memories and reactions. These parents desire closeness with others, but are very fearful due to their own unresolved traumatic experiences. They are the most likely to respond with the fight, flight or freeze reaction in the face of their child's distress. These parents are most likely to be unable to maintain emotional connection to the child when the child is distressed. They may identify too strongly with the child and re-experience their own feelings of being a victim. They may also feel victimized by the child's anger, identifying the child with their former abuser. These parents must have their own therapy for trauma or loss before they can help their children heal. Parents with an unresolved, fearful style of attachment have a much greater chance of having children with a disorganized attachment style, unless the parents can reach greater levels of security themselves.

Putting it all in perspective

So what are parents to do when faced with the residues of their own attachment styles and the challenges of raising a child with serious attachment difficulties? First, parents must recognize that we all are shaped by the legacy of our early experiences. Hopefully, this can give parents new insight into, and compassion for, the struggle the child faces. If it is hard for us to change, when we may have only had some insecure attachment styles, how hard must it be for these children with disorders of attachment? Second, it can help us predict what our vulnerabilities may be, so that we can more easily recognize "red flags" that could interfere with the secure attachment experiences we are trying to create for our children. Third, it can help us understand that acquired or achieved security is possible—for ourselves and for our children. This is not a quick fix. It is a journey of rediscovery of who we are, what motivates us, what we missed, what we need, and what we hope for. It is the honoring of all that has shaped us, and of our ability to accept all and still choose the best. We will stumble along the way, but we can also pick ourselves up and continue on—learning new things about ourselves each time. Many parents find that, in helping their children to heal, they learn as much about themselves as they do about their child. They learn that issues they thought were resolved were actually only partially resolved. While this can be unsettling for awhile, it can also continually remind us of how powerful are the "handprints on the heart" that parents leave. When resolved fully, these experiences leave us with greater resilience to face future challenges. Fourth, we can recognize that we are all human, and all trying to do the best we can, wherever we are at a particular time. When the challenges are too much and the load too heavy, we can ask for help. For, as the old Irish proverb goes, "It is in the shelter of others that we all live and grow."

Resources for this chapter:

Main, M., Kaplan, N., Cassidy, J., (1985). *Security in infancy, childhood, and adulthood: A move to the level of representation*. Monographs of the Society for Research in Child Development, 50, 66 - 104.

Robert Karen, *On Becoming Attached: First Relationships and How They Shape Our Capacity to Love.*

Daniel Siegel, *The Developing Mind: How Relationships and the Brain Shape Who We Are (1999)*

Daniel Siegel and Mary Hartzell, *Parenting From the Inside Out (2004).*

CHAPTER 3

Therapeutic Parenting

This chapter explains the principles that are keys to successfully parenting children who have disorders of attachment, and how to apply these principles to real-life parenting challenges. Because the academic and professional thinking about disorders of attachment, attachment therapy and, thus, attachment parenting[1] have evolved and changed rather dramatically over the past few decades, this chapter begins with a brief history to provide context for the current thinking.

A brief history of attachment therapy

In the 1970s, a new treatment approach was developed for children who had histories of maltreatment and loss and who were resistant to traditional forms of therapy. This approach was called Rage Reduction Therapy (Zaslow & Menta, 1975), and included catharsis, provocation of rage, and intense confrontation.

1. Attachment Parenting International.

Over the next two decades, findings in the fields of trauma, neuroscience and attachment began to discredit those coercive approaches (Kelly, 2003), supporting instead therapeutic approaches that emphasize sensitivity and attunement. Examples of such therapy include narrative therapies, some play therapies, and other methodologies focused on increased emotional regulation and trauma processing.

In 2003, ATTACh officially separated itself from its early roots and embraced the current prevailing thinking about effective, appropriate treatment of children with disorders of attachment in its first position paper, *ATTACh Position Statement on Coercive Therapy.* The current white paper on this subject (2006) is available on the ATTACh website (attach.org), and parents are encouraged to read it.

The principles presented in this chapter are based on the current thinking about attachment therapy, as described in ATTACh's position statement. As research in the field of attachment continues to yield deeper understanding of these complex issues, ATTACh will continue to evolve its positions and practices accordingly.

Regulation and dysregulation

Attachment parenting requires an understanding of the concepts of regulation and dysregulation. These terms refer to the physical and emotional state of the child:

- Regulated—able to flexibly experience, tolerate, and manage a range of emotions, both positive (e.g., joy, excitement) and negative (e.g., sadness, fear) without becoming overwhelmed, and is able to easily regain an emotional balance in which he or she is calm, receptive, and able to process thoughts and feelings
- Dysregulated—in an overwhelmed, overwrought state

Research has shown that children learn best during times when they are regulated (Schore, 2001). But children who have experienced attachment-related traumas often are very easily triggered into a powerful dysregulated state. Some children have lived in these fearful, agitated states so long that the "states have become traits" (Bruce Perry).

What these children need is active, helpful, empathic assistance in transitioning to a calmer state. When parents provide that kind of help, they are providing critically important corrective emotional experiences for their children. But it's no easy task—children are often most resistant to this help when they most need it. Indeed, their distorted perceptions and negative beliefs often cause them to quite literally misperceive the intention of help and resist it.

What would you do?

Amy was at her wits end. They had to leave for the airport in an hour and there was still so much to do! Instructions for the dog sitter, garbage out, medications to pack...and the kids had been bickering constantly since the moment they woke up. Amy wanted to sit down and cry. Just then a football came sailing into the kitchen, knocking a glass of orange juice off the kitchen table on its way.

Some possible endings:

A—Amy stormed into the next room screaming, "Who threw that football?!?" The boys both pointed to each other saying "He did." One child poked the other as he was pointing at him, and received a hard punch on the arm from his brother in return. Amy grabbed both boys and dragged them to the couch, putting them at opposite ends. "Don't MOVE!" she screamed, giving them "the eye," and stomped back to the kitchen to resume her tasks.

B—Amy walked into the next room, and calmly said, "I don't care who threw that football, but both of you need to clean up the mess, now." One boy whined, "But I didn't DO anything." The other one whined louder, "You did TOO, I'm not cleaning up your mess." Amy calmly said, "When the mess is cleaned up, we'll leave. I sure hope we don't miss the plane, though, because then you'll have to buy us all new tickets, and that will take months and months of chores!" Amy resumed her tasks.

Most parents would probably respond as Amy did in Scenario A, acting on emotion and instinct. However, this approach is guaranteed to escalate the situation into a full-blown power struggle, prolonging the children's state of dysregulation and, thus, the misbehavior. It is also likely to incite real fear in the children, as the physical nature of the intervention may trigger memories of earlier trauma.

Scenario B is a better choice, as Amy's calm reaction should help the children move to a more regulated state. Backing off when a child escalates helps to create an atmosphere of safety and trust that is the basis for attachment to occur, and helps the child learn to regulate himself. However, as implemented in this scenario, it is purely a behavioral intervention, designed to obtain the desired results of getting the orange juice cleaned up and helping the children learn to take responsibility for their actions using logical consequences.

As you'll see in the next section, there is an even more therapeutic approach.

Attunement and empathy

Even the most sensitive, nurturing, well-intended intervention can backfire with a child who has a disorder of attachment. The parent must work hard to help the child make sense of the experience by verbalizing her intentions, explaining the child's reactions, and reassuring the child. Navigating through these episodes is one of the hardest things parents ever have to do. To be successful, it is critical that the parents maintain a position of being "bigger, stronger, and wiser"[2] with their power always fueled by empathy for how hard it is to be the child, and by a hope that real healing is possible.

Consider the following response to the orange juice spill described in the previous section:

Scenario C—Amy walked into the room where the children were playing and said, "Oh my gosh! You guys spilled the orange juice! You are really bouncing off the walls this morning! You must be excited to go on this trip, huh? And maybe a little scared, since the last time you were on a plane was when you left Russia. Come on - let's all get this orange juice cleaned up, then I want you to go outside and shoot some baskets until we leave.That should help you calm down and feel less nervous. I'll tell you what - whoever gets the most baskets before we leave gets to choose their seat on the airplane first!"

This scenario not only helps the children move toward a more regulated state, but verbalizes the feelings they are likely having and demonstrates empathy for them. By working together to clean up the mess, Amy clearly positions herself on the children's side, rather than ending up on opposing sides of a power struggle.

Consider another typical scenario:

2. Robert Marvin, Circle of Security.

What would you do?

Margaret's grandson, Tony, came to visit for Father's Day weekend. Shortly after he arrived, he showed Margaret the spending money he had brought with him. Margaret told Tony he wouldn't need any money that weekend, as they would be spending Saturday preparing for a Father's Day celebration on Sunday, and to put his money back into his suitcase. Tony set his jaw and loudly refused.

Some possible endings:

Scenario A—Margaret took Tony's money away from him and put it away in his suitcase. Tony immediately had a meltdown, and began running through the house with his sleeping bag, knocking things over as he went, and screaming, "I never want to come here again!" Margaret took the sleeping bag away from him, which enraged him further. Tony escalated into a full-blown rage.

Scenario B—Margaret realized that Tony was on the verge of a meltdown, and said, "I was just thinking that your money would be safer in your suitcase, but if you want to hang onto it that's your choice, I just hope you don't lose it. It sure would take a lot of chores to earn all that money back." She then left him alone to play with some toys (watching from the next room), and he eventually calmed down. He even wrote her an apology note for refusing to follow directions.

Scenario C—Margaret said, "I bet that's disappointing for you because you have been looking forward to shopping with your money and it's so hard to wait longer. But I know you love your grandpa and we want to do something really special for him since it's Father's Day. You know, that reminds me of a story I know...there once was this boy named Josh, who got $50 for his birthday and couldn't wait to spend it..." Margaret went on to tell the impromptu story of Josh and all of the obstacles that stood in the way of him spending his birthday money, and how he survived them until that one wonderful day his Mom took him on a shopping spree.

Hopefully it's becoming clear how critical it is to both the short- and long-term success of attachment parenting interventions that parents focus on helping a child move toward a regulated state, remaining attuned to his emotional needs, and communicating empathy.

Coercion

The definition of coercion contained in Merriam-Webster's Dictionary is, "the use of expressed or implied threats of violence or reprisal...or other intimidating behavior that puts a person in immediate fear of the consequences in order to compel that person to act against his or her will." In simpler terms, getting a person to act against his will out of fear (of consequences, violence, etc.).

The use of any coercive approach to parenting interferes with the goal of creating a secure parent-child relationship characterized by safety, reciprocal love, trust, and perceived security.

Parenting strategies such as logical and reasonable consequences, enforcing limits, and so on may appear at first glance to fit the definition of coercive. But, because they are not (typically) accompanied by fear, these are legitimate interventions when used in the context of a loving parent/child relationship.

As a matter of policy and practice, ATTACh does not support and indeed actively discourages the use of coercion in treatment. ATTACh does not condone its members, registered clinicians, registered agencies, or presenters using coercive therapies or parenting techniques. This position is detailed in ATTACh's White Paper on Coercion (attach.org).

Physical containment

When addressing physical containment, it is important to distinguish between:

- Physical containment in the form of minimally necessary force used to stop aggression or destruction in the interest of safety, and
- Physical containment used as a therapeutic or parenting strategy.

The use of minimally necessary force for safety

People who have experienced trauma may be vulnerable to intrusive thoughts or feelings related to the unresolved trauma. When this happens, they respond in unconscious and emotionally reactive ways. Some children, when triggered into a state of severe dysregulation, quickly escalate into a violent rage, endangering themselves and the people around them. In this case, physical containment by a parent trained in using a containment strategy is clearly in the best interest of the child. However, such containment should always be performed in as minimally invasive a manner as is effective, by a parent who is in control of his or her own emotions. The parent must be able to maintain an empathetic demeanor during the containment, and the containment should only last as long as is necessary to ensure a safe environment. Further, the parent should ensure that the child understands what is happening, so the containment is not perceived as being hurtful (e.g., "We are keeping you safe until you can get your control back.") Parents need professional training in safe restraint techniques in order to implement this intervention safely and effectively.

The use of physical containment as a therapeutic or parenting strategy

The appropriateness of physical containment as a strategy for helping a child move from dysregulation to regulation must be determined for each child individually—there is no "one size fits all" answer to this question.

Some children need, and can accept, physical containment through being held lovingly in their parents' arms to get to a calmer state. Other children become even more agitated and aggressive with any form of touch. In this case, until the child's traumatic triggers are resolved, this form of physical containment does not work and may be dangerous if the child continues to escalate. Still other children freeze and/or dissociate during physical interventions—while they may appear calmer on the outside, on the inside they are in a terrified, dysregulated state.

It is critical to understand where the child is on the regulation/dysregulation continuum when assessing the appropriateness of physical containment. This understanding comes through attunement with the child over time, as the parent learns the child's signals and/or cues and develops a more sensitive and responsive relationship with the child.

Minimizing trauma during temporary separations

As hard as you try, there are times when you simply have to leave your child with someone else, if only for a few hours or overnight. This can be a stressful time in the life of a child with attachment issues. Attachment-related traumas can impair the child's ability to internalize a parent/caregiver, which enables the child to trust that the relationship continues even during absences. For many children, the most difficult period of experiencing separation is when they are actually in the healing process and have begun to experience both the joys and the inevitable vulnerability of feeling attached to a safe person who returns their love.

Hopefully, you will not need to be apart from your child often. But for those times that you do, here are some ways to help your child through the separation:

- Allow your child to sleep with your pillow, or even in your bed, while you are away.
- Leave an audio or video tape of you reading a favorite bed-time story, for the child to listen to while you are gone.
- Wear your own favorite T-shirt or sleepwear and then, without washing it, leave it for your child to take to bed or when he or she misses you.
- Take a picture or drawing of you and your child together with you, and make sure he knows you will keep it close to you while you are gone. Do the same for your child, but be aware that he may "lose" it if he is angry about being separated from you.
- Prepare notes or "secret messages" for your child to open while you are away. Emphasize that you are thinking of her at the very moment she is reading it, and that you miss her as much as she misses you.
- Decide ahead of time when you will be able to phone your child. Make sure the caregiver arranges for your child to be home at that time so he does not miss your call.

- Make sure your child's caregiver is aware of the problems that can be stirred up by your absence. Distraction can help an emotionally upset child; the caregiver can take the child to a favorite place, restaurant, or the library, or can read a favorite book endless times.
- Plan a celebration to mark your return. It should be quiet, without too many people around, and should focus on attachment-type activities that you have already found soothing to your child.

If you leave your child in therapeutic respite care, at a babysitter's house, or at a day-care center, remember that he will have pent-up frustrations and fear from the entire day. When you arrive at the end of your time away, and before you leave the sitter's home or day-care center, let the child process those feelings. Reassure him that you are back. Hold him, sit with him, let him spend five or ten minutes working through reconnecting. Apologize for having left him but explain that you will never leave him for more time than he can handle. This should not be "putting on your coat and gathering up your things" time, but quiet time when you can sit, relax, hold each other, and look into his eyes as he lets you know he is angry at your leaving him. It really works, sometimes not in five minutes in the beginning, but he eventually learns how to throw his worry and anger out in his "trash can" at the door, leaving his anxiety there. The two of you can then go home together in a happy, connected spirit.

This section was based on the book Becoming a Family, Promoting Healthy Attachments with Your Adopted Child, by Lark Eshleman, Ph.D.

Q & A

It is not easy for parents of children who have disorders of attachment to truly internalize the principles described in this chapter (and in more detail in ATTACh's White Paper on Coercion). This section addresses some of the questions that you may have regarding the application of these principles.

Q. Our children are doing all kinds of inappropriate and even hurtful behaviors. Are you saying we can't confront or punish those behaviors?

A. Clearly adults, especially parents, have a responsibility to help guide and socialize children so that they learn which behaviors are expected and effective. The White Paper seeks to distinguish between confrontation done in a safe and ultimately therapeutic way, versus a more coercive and potentially harmful way. Children who have been traumatized tend to respond in reactive and defensive ways. If we view that as purely defiant behavior, this can lead to coercive interventions to make the child comply. We may briefly end the behavior, but may unintentionally reinforce the child's belief that others are essentially controlling versus helpful. This works against the formation of secure attachment. If, however, we try to look beneath the behavior and appreciate what might trigger the response, we can better deal with the behavior and what is driving it! Attachment-focused therapy is most effective when it revises the distorted beliefs of the child's internal working model. Behavioral interventions alone don't realize the same long-term results. It is important to distinguish between punishment and consequences. Punishment is designed to make the child suffer for his offenses; consequences are the result of the child's choices or actions. Punishment more often teaches children not to get caught. Consequences used with empathy help children truly internalize our guidance and values. **Connections, not compliance, are the keystone for success. It is through connections that compliance evolves.**

Q. Does this mean I can never forcibly hold my child? What if she is trying to hurt me or someone else?

A. Perhaps no area has been more controversial over the years than holding a child. For many, holding has been synonymous with attachment therapy. In the new paradigm of ATTACh, many interventions are used that do not involve holding in any way. Nonetheless, nurturing, loving touch is an essential component of normal parent-child interaction.

ATTACh supports nurturing and loving interactions, whether they occur in normal parenting or in a therapeutic setting, when no coercion of any kind is involved.

ATTACh opposes any and all forms of holding that does involve coercion, and that is intended to bring about a rage in a child until he "breaks through" to a calmer state.

An important distinction needs to be made when a child requires forcible restraint because she is at a risk of hurting herself, others, or damaging property. Such restraint is intended to be a temporary safety measure, and is not by itself therapeutic. Restraint should be terminated as soon as safety can be maintained without it, and special care must be exercised to ensure the safety of the child and adult(s) involved in the restraint. The use of restraint is governed by national and local laws; adults should familiarize themselves with the laws and their implications, and should be professionally trained in the use of safe restraint.

Q. So if I set a limit with my child and he explodes, have I "intentionally dysregulated" him? You want me to sympathize with a child who just hit me? How am I supposed to parent?

A. This is what makes the explanation of this paradigm shift so difficult! Of course, many children with traumatic backgrounds react explosively to limits, and we don't mean that you should never set a limit that results in an explosion. We are not advocating in any way that parents should walk on eggshells, fearing to set reasonable limits. What we are saying is that, as you get to know your child's reactions to limits, you also work to find ways to set reasonable limits that will be minimally dysregulating. As you and your child learn to co-regulate his emotions, his explosive outbursts will decrease. If your child is very reactive, you will need to decide how to be safe and help your child learn to find regulation and comfort in your parenting.

When a child reacts explosively to a simple limit, it is important to look at what is fueling that explosion. What kinds of limits were placed on your child in the past and how were they enforced?

- Did his former parents or caregivers set limits arbitrarily and explosively themselves?
- Was your child likely to be shamed, beaten, or isolated for long periods?

- Did your child end up learning the lesson that doing something wrong could be life-threatening?
- Did anyone help your child re-regulate his overwhelming emotions after being punished?
- Did anyone ever help him learn to manage difficult feelings at all?
- When he did something wrong, did he end up feeling guilty (e.g., "I did something wrong and need to change that")? Or, did making a mistake cause him to feel deep shame (e.g., "I am bad, and there is no point in trying to change")?

Your child may have experienced limits and punishments as terrifying, and possibly life-threatening or deeply shaming. If he was not taught to manage emotions and arousal from the very earliest days of life, then your child may not have any tools to deal with the fear or internal arousal he experiences when you say, "no." In fact, any limit may be a trigger for earlier traumatic experiences of limits, and when a child is experiencing a traumatic re-triggering he is not capable of being reasoned with, only soothed and comforted. Even small cues may elicit a post-traumatic reaction from our children. These can include an even slightly raised voice, a request to go to his room to calm down, or even a frown. None of this means that limits aren't necessary—only that we need to become expert "readers" of our children's cues as to the meaning of their behavior. Parents need to find the "therapeutic window" (Briere) where the child is available to learn, not when he is so aroused that any teaching or comfort is rejected.

Let's sort out the components that go into "appropriate" responses to parental limits. First, there is the teaching of emotion regulation, which occurs in healthy development thousands of times during the first years of life. Every time you say to a baby, "Don't worry, Mommy is going to feed you/ pick you up/ clean your bottom," that baby learns that things aren't as bad as they seemed, and that there are solutions to life's most difficult situations. The child is learning two important lessons: 1) that negative feelings can be tolerated because they don't last long and 2) help is always available. These are the foundations of the important skill of frustration tolerance and cause-and-effect thinking. By the time that baby is six months old, the sound of your voice will calm him before you've even opened his door. By the time he's three, tantrums will be milder than they were before, because he's learned that when Mom or Dad insist on limits, they aren't going to give up, and that he is still a child who is loved, even if he doesn't like the limits. Children who have not learned this tend to react strongly because they think the word "no" means that they are bad.

Shame is an important element when children overreact to limits. A child whose needs haven't been met and considered important, who hasn't been the apple of someone's eye, and who may have been punished arbitrarily, or for expressing normal needs such as hunger, will have learned at an early age that he is not worth much to others. He will adopt the same feeling about himself and about others. **Every "no" will reinforce this feeling of deep shame about the self, and will likely incur fury.** Shame, coupled with chronic frustration of needs, can lead to rage. At a very minimum, it will increase dysregulation. Contrast this child with the one whose needs are met, who is valued, and whose parents explain that although limits are necessary, they don't value the child any less for transgressing them. That child will experience "healthy" shame, which is brief and serves as a prompt to change future behavior, but won't experience the corrosive and all-encompassing shame of the first child.

Another important element to consider when attempting to understand a child's reaction to limits is the meaning of the limit to the child. If you have been away from your child, he may be particularly sensitive to any "no" because of a reawakening of early abandonment/shame feelings. Then, if you suggest that you can't play with him because you have to take care of the baby, **the fury which ensues may be related to the child's earlier, real abandonment, not the small one he has just experienced**. If you realize that your child will typically be much more sensitive after a separation, you may be able to avoid putting him in the position of having to share your attention. If you can't avoid it, your reaction will be very different than if you look at his response as totally out of line with the limit placed. React by holding him and comforting him with your understanding that it is very hard to share after you have been away, because old feelings of being unlovable, rejected or even abandoned may have resurfaced. When comforting is coupled with putting words to the child's feelings, you not only reduce the length and intensity of that outburst, but you begin to build an internal understanding that he isn't bad and deserving of abandonment, just needy, and those needs will be met.

A final important piece of the puzzle is to consider your child's internal working model of attachment. A child with a background of maltreatment learns that she is not lovable, that the caregiving environment is not predictable and nurturing, and that the world is a scary place. Let's say your child has learned that not only is she bad, but she is not going to get what she wants. Now, when you say "no" to a request of ice cream before dinner, those primal feelings of need, and of the likelihood that those needs will not be met, may erupt to overwhelm both of you. After a few of these experiences, you will have learned that your response should be to offer a small snack with your explanation that you will show her the ice cream, which is reserved for after dinner. You may find that your child is less upset with this approach. If you do this many times, with explanations that, in your home, you will always be sure she is fed, those explosions will likely diminish over time.

Q. The attachment therapy we received was the only thing that helped my child. Are you trying to take away the very thing that saved my child?

A. Many parents and therapists have shared poignant stories of how attachment therapies focused on holding and other highly confrontational methods helped their children, when other, more traditional, therapies had not. Our purpose is not to negate those outcomes. Rather, we now know that many children are being helped with less intrusive methods. This causes us to reconsider the assumptions on which the more confrontational methods were based. Confrontational holding therapies were premised on the idea that children had hardened defenses, which had to be "broken down" before the child could connect. The use of confrontation in many areas of therapy (including with sex offenders and substance abusers, who have very hardened defenses) has been challenged and has ultimately proven less effective. Just as science has moved surgery from very intrusive operations with huge scars to minimally intrusive procedures covered by small bandages, so has brain research helped us find less intrusive ways to gain access to a defensive child, thereby helping to move that child toward better emotional functioning.

Q. Are you saying that we can't use psychodrama and other techniques to help our child?

A. Psychodrama, story-telling in the form of life-books, narrative therapy, and other techniques can be very useful to help children process and make sense of their history and related feelings. Moreover, such techniques can be used for many reasons, including to facilitate attunement and to enhance a child's sense of security and safety.

We need all the tools in our boxes to help children really process both the memory and the feelings related to the trauma. But there are good reasons why a child has built defenses, consciously or unconsciously, in the first place. These defenses helped him survive the trauma, or were developed in response to the trauma to help him adapt, but may no longer make sense in the context of a nurturing caregiver. However, such strategies are very difficult to relinquish, when experience has taught that they were necessary to survive. They can be modified only as the child learns new coping skills.

We must respect the reasons these strategies were developed in the first place. To change these strategies, children need new and different experiences that teach them it is safe to relinquish defensive strategies and begin to embrace the nurturing and help that are now available. Adults who are sensitive and respectful in exploration of traumatic memories and gentle, yet firm in setting limits, will provide powerful experiences to challenge the child's beliefs that others are hurtful, coercive, etc. These new experiences will create new beliefs: others can understand her feelings, exploration is safe in the presence of a compassionate caregiver, and emotional sharing leads to healing.

The concept of a **"therapeutic window,"** as described in our White Paper, is a very important one here. What we have learned from recent work in the neurosciences is that therapy is best accomplished when the client is adequately "alive" to the situation being discussed. The client benefits most when having access to both the ideas and feelings related to the situation, but not having to experience the full intensity of early traumatic memories and feelings. The trauma may have never been resolved because the client has been too fearful to re-experience the life-threatening strength of the original event. Simply going back there would only reinforce the trauma. When trauma is experienced, our brain makes use of its most primitive skills, those that assist us to fight, flee, or freeze. When our brain is in this mode, it shuts down more advanced brain functions—those that would allow us to understand how those experiences might have affected us, those that would allow us to see how we might understand it differently now, and those that would allow us actually to reprocess the trauma, emerging with new meaning, new understanding, and new feelings. We must go back to resolve it, but in going back, we need to find ways to limit its strength. If we do this, the child will have access to all levels of brain functioning, and will be able to reduce the strength of the reaction as well as learn new skills for dealing with other difficult memories. If we don't tame the triggers first, then we risk reactivating and reinforcing the very fear circuit in the brain that kept the child stuck in the fearful, defensive, survival reaction.

A therapist who is aware of the need to maintain the child within the therapeutic window will be noticing, in the moment, how the child is reacting to each suggestion, question, or other intervention the therapist uses. When there is an indication that the child is moved by a particular thought or event, the therapist can begin the exploration with care to prevent overwhelming him. When the child shows indications of being overwhelmed, which will break the trusting rapport, the therapist will move back to repair the break and to understand better what may have caused the strong reaction. The lesson learned by the child is that the therapist is sensitive to his feelings, can understand why the situation became difficult, and will protect the child from being overwhelmed again. The child is much more likely to trust that therapist to explore new areas in the future than he would trust a therapist who pushed on to reach a resolution, which might have had meaning for the therapist but which would have been hollow for the child.

Q. We have a 13-year old boy who is physically aggressive with Mom. What do we do about his pushing and shoving?

A: The ideal place to begin is *before* the situation has reached this point. Uncovering the meaning of the behavior...what is driving it (fear, dissociation, fright about something, flash-back, etc.)... is crucial. **Trying to stop a surface behavior is rarely effective in the long run, if the goal is developing an internal, self-directed sense of control.** So, begin by exploring what provokes these episodes and begin way before the aggression is evident. How and when is there a beginning escalation? The other advantage of doing this is that the increase in parental sensitivity, attunement and responsiveness will pay loads of dividends in other interactions.

Unfortunately, many children will dysregulate no matter how good you are at attuning. Sometimes it's because they're afraid of getting close and beginning to trust. Sometimes it's because you or someone else has triggered a traumatic memory. Sometimes you never figure it out. After the fact, the most important thing is not to allow yourself to dysregulate as much as your child has. You need to make sure she has a way of calming, and whether it means restraint, going into her room, holding her on your lap, or sending her out to play in the yard is something each parent has to figure out with each child. The message she needs to receive is that you are able to be calm, you know she will be able to calm down too, and you will help her if necessary.

Consequences are another issue. After a disruptive episode, parents sometimes want to retaliate, even more so if their child has destroyed things or hurt someone. Still, the thing we hope for, more than anything else, is that the child will learn new skills to manage his feelings. So, consequences should always be focused on teaching the child. Think about ways to help your child learn while he is also making amends. First, if he is truly sorry, he should apologize. Then, if he has destroyed something, perhaps he should do chores to earn the money to replace the item (or often just replace part of it). Or, if he has hurt and frightened Mom, he should do something for her—perhaps some of her chores, and make her a cup of tea to have while he is doing chores. Talking this through also helps with development of conscience and empathy ("This really hurt Mom and scared her, and she felt bad for a while—that means I should do something nice for her.") If the impetus for the outburst was that the child was being reminded for the umpteenth time to do something he hadn't done, then the child, if old enough, should do some things under supervision to help him better learn to follow directions. Sometimes it is difficult to think of a good consequence. It is OK to take some time and think it through. Consequences do not have to be immediate. Indeed, the parent modeling the process of calming down and truly thinking about things is important in teaching children how to do this! Remember that the goal is to help the child develop some new brain wiring which will make it possible for him to learn to control his temper. Always look for a "teachable moment" when you can help your child to learn or refine a skill.

One of the most important teachable moments is actually teaching the child that mistakes can be overcome and breaks in relationships can be repaired. These experiences powerfully challenge the child's distorted beliefs, such as "I am no good," "Others always leave me," and "Life isn't fair." Learning how to repair relationships is one of the most critical skills we can have in being able to maintain relationships. Many children with attachment disorders never learned this.

CHAPTER 4

Parent Practice from A to Z

This chapter discusses how to apply the principles described in the previous chapter to everyday parenting challenges. **It is not our intention to provide a one-size-fits-all solution to any given situation, but rather to help you internalize the spirit of attachment parenting principles, so that you can develop your own successful interventions for your child.**

Scenario A: You are talking on the phone. Your child continually interrupts you by asking you questions and doing things she knows she is not allowed to do (taking candy from the candy dish, throwing a ball across the house). What do you do?

Possible cause: She feels ignored, which may trigger memories of neglect or abandonment. She may also be jealous of the caller, who is receiving your attention.

Suggested intervention: When you are not on the phone, teach her that, when you are making a call, she should touch your arm (gently) to let you know that she needs your attention. When she does so, smile, make eye contact, and let her know that you will give her your full attention as soon as the phone call has ended.

Scenario B: You are at a restaurant and your child pitches a fit because you won't let him order what he wants. He is talking loudly and banging his head on the booth. What do you do?

Possible cause: His blood sugar may be low, or his hunger may remind him of having been deprived of food during his earlier years.

Suggested intervention: First, remove him from the situation by taking him to the car or to a restroom. Try to soothe him. Once he can listen, talk about what food means to him. Let him know that, in your family, there will *always* be enough healthy food to nourish his body. Some families solve this problem by ordering the same meal for all of their children every time they eat in a restaurant.

Scenario C: Your two children are arguing over what TV channel to watch. What do you do?

Possible cause: Both children want to watch what they are interested in watching, and it is not the same. They may be engaging in a power struggle for dominance and control, or they may want to get your attention.

Suggested intervention: Ideally, their choice should be negotiated before the television is turned on. Tell them, in a calm voice, that you want to help them find a show they can both enjoy. If the television is on, turn it off, sit down with them, and help them problem solve. Keep the television off until they can reach an agreement. The sooner they agree, the sooner they can watch. If they can't agree, you choose a show.

Scenario D: Your child is arguing with you in the grocery store because she wants you to buy her a candy bar. She's starting to make a scene. What do you do?

Possible cause: She may be hungry, thirsty, tired, or ill. Or perhaps, as you become more task-focused and less attuned to your child, she feels more insecure. Old insecurities meant she didn't feel lovable, worthy, or important. Instead of being able to verbalize her fears, she demands concrete "proof" that her needs matter.

Suggested intervention: It is important to recognize that most children do not like to go grocery shopping, especially if they are hungry, thirsty, tired, ill or have been restricted from physical activity for a prolonged period of time and are restless (for example if they've been in school all day and you pick them up to go shopping). Anticipating problems ahead of time and making sure your child is fed, has a snack, is well rested and understands what you must purchase at the store before entering the store creates a win-win situation. If you must continue shopping, it is often helpful to negotiate a win-win situation that is acceptable to you at the time ("You can choose a candy bar but you cannot eat it until after dinner") or, if your child's behavior escalates and negotiation is not possible, you can leave the store without buying anything and return alone. It is important to give your child another opportunity to comply in the grocery store if you must leave and return alone. Praise your child during the next shopping trip to reinforce the behavior you want. Allow her to help get items when possible, and confirm for your child that you don't particularly like grocery shopping either but you both have to eat!

Scenario E: You ask your child to unload the dishwasher and he rolls his eyes, whining, "Why do I always have to unload the dishwasher?" What do you do?

Possible cause: He is doing something else and does not want to stop what he is doing to do his chore. He could be bored with doing the dishes, or he could be tired.

Suggested intervention: Chores are an important part of daily life, and your child should be able to participate in chores without whining. All children whine some of the time. Setting up clear expectations about when and how the chore will be done creates a predictable routine for your child. For example you can tell him that when the dishes are put away you will be able to start cooking dinner. You can give more responsibility by telling your child that the dishes must be put away before 4 PM (assuming he comes home from school at 3 PM, that gives him time to unwind and then do the chore). Ignore the whining and set the timer to see if he can get all the dishes put away before the timer goes off (set it for 5 - 10 minutes, which is plenty of time to put dishes away). Always praise your child for a job well done. It might be worth considering other chores for variety. Some children respond well to a "Day Off" card that they can choose to use at will (once per week), as it increases their sense of having some control and can reduce resistance.

Scenario F: You find an electronic device in your child's room that is not hers. What do you do?

Possible cause: This could have been an impulsive act, when she wanted the item and took it without thinking. She may also have "known" that you would never allow her to have it because, in her belief system, she is unlovable and adults never care. She may have been angry at the owner of the item, and took it to punish that person. She may have traded another item for this one, or it may have been a gift or a loan from another child.

Suggested intervention: The first thing is to try to understand your child's point of view, feelings, and thoughts. While you might *assume* that she stole the item, that may or may not be true. Even if it is true, focusing on that aspect does not lead you to understand the reasons behind the behavior. We want to address those, not merely the surface behavior. You might first show your child what you found and say, in a calm and interested voice (tone of voice and cadence are crucial here), "I found this in your room. What's the story here?" Then, "accept" whatever the child says and continue asking questions (not to "get the truth", but to demonstrate that you are interested in your child and how she feels, thinks, and views the world). Also, avoiding highly charged words such as "stealing," and using reframed expressions such as "using without permission," can help defuse the reaction so that more discussion is possible.

Scenario G: When you ask your child how his day was, he says he had a good day at school. A half hour later you get a call from the school principal telling you that your son hit another student during recess. What do you do?

Possible causes:

Fear. He may be afraid of your reaction because he assumes that you will be angry and punitive as previous parents have been. He may feel unlovable and not valued. This leads to him "knowing" that you will be angry and punish him, even if the action was provoked.

Shame: He may have acted impulsively, and is now ashamed of his actions. Young children hide when they feel shame. Older children can be more sophisticated and act as if the action never occurred (another way of hiding).

Suggested intervention: Begin by assuming some level of shame and fear. You might say, "I'm sorry you didn't feel you could tell me what happened at school today. Maybe you still don't trust me, and worry that I will be angry at you and be mean like others have been. Tell me what happened. The principal said __________________. How do you remember it?"

Scenario H: When you give your child a consequence, she runs away from you. What do you do?

Possible cause: Your child may be impulsive, contrary, tired, and probably developmentally unable to self-regulate her behavior. Most children test limits some of the time.

Suggested intervention: If this happens consistently, it might be time to change the consequence and evaluate the behavior depending on the age of your child. Most children understand that poor behavior will require a consequence. However, children with disorders of attachment may have very distorted beliefs about this. They may not have experienced good parenting role models. Sometimes they need explicit instructions, such as, "good moms/dads help their kids learn the right thing by teaching them right from wrong." Some children respond well to agreeing ahead of time what the consequence will be for specific behaviors, and they will complete the consequence (albeit grudgingly). Try working toward a better understanding of the negative behavior. If running away from you presents a safety risk, take all precautions to contain your child for his own safety.

Scenario I: Your child chatters non-stop in the car, asking nonsense questions and pointing out everything he sees. You are so distracted that it is interfering with your driving. What do you do?

Possible cause: Your child is probably experiencing some anxiety, perhaps some fear, or may be simply seeking attention. His anxiety may be fueled by the fact that you cannot give him your undivided attention. If he is feeling fearful, the chattering could be his way of distracting himself from experiencing this feeling. Chattering can be a way to literally "turn on" parts of the brain that help the child soothe himself in the face of intensely distressing feelings.

Suggested intervention: Remember that the only person's behavior you can control is your own! If you are not too far from your destination, you might just acknowledge that your son is talking, and just stay focused on reaching your destination. If you have a long drive ahead, be sure to keep things in the car that could distract him, possibly music (his own CD player with earplugs) or soft cover books (in case he throws them). If these diversions are ineffective, stop at a safe place, take a break, and acknowledge that your child really wants to talk. Keep a kitchen timer in the car, and set it for a certain amount of minutes. Offer your child the opportunity to talk while you give him your undivided attention. At the end of the allotted time period, put your earplug in one ear with your music and move on with the trip. Another strategy is to see if you can engage your child in singing with you.

If you have tried all of these techniques and they are still not effective, he is probably not capable of dealing with long trips. If you cannot leave him at home the next time, it would be best to postpone future trips.

Scenario J: You are at a birthday party and your child starts running around wildly, pushing and shoving and yelling. What do you do?

Possible cause: She may feel nervous in this new environment and not know how to contain her anxiety. She may be feeling overwhelmed and over-stimulated in this birthday party setting. She may also be having a hard time not being the center of attention, and is probably jealous of the birthday boy or girl.

Suggested intervention: Keep yourself calm! Breathe. Don't personalize her behavior. Provide some physical/environmental containment to help her calm down. Keep in close proximity of your child so you can be a buffer to stimulation—take her outdoors or into a calm area so that she can get re-regulated. Give her the language to express how she is feeling. If all else fails, remove her from the party (just politely thank the hostess and leave before your child has a complete meltdown). If you need to leave early, don't present it to your child as a punishment, but rather, "I can see by your behavior that this is difficult for you to be here, so let's leave now."

Scenario K: You are at church and your child keeps talking to you and kicking the chair in front of him. What do you do?

Possible cause: He may be bored at church and wants a distraction. He may be seeking attention (if positive attention is not being given, he will try for negative attention). He may have trouble sitting still due to neurological reasons such as ADHD.

Suggested intervention: Remove him from the sanctuary, or move to the back of the church to a seat where he cannot disturb anyone. Hold him on your lap. Bring a few small toys that he is only allowed to play with during church, not at any other time during the week.

Scenario L: Your child wants a cookie, but you say "no" because it's almost dinner time. She starts yelling at you, calling you every name she can think of. What do you do?

Possible cause: Her blood sugar may be low and she is feeling tired and grouchy. She may have a difficult time deferring gratification in general, or may be distressed about something unrelated. She may be seeking a power struggle (to discharge negative energy) and this may be the "perfect" set up.

Suggested intervention: Keep yourself calm. Breathe. Don't personalize behavior. Don't react to the content of your child's words. Respond with something like, "Sounds as though you're feeling cranky right now," and then attempt to figure out what is going on with her. Assess if she may just be hungry and have low blood sugar, and then offer her the option of another, healthier snack. You can say something like, "Wow, you have not eaten in a long time and must be so hungry. Those big hungry feelings are making you act really grouchy. Here, let me give you a snack to help you feel better."

Depending on your child and your own personal tolerance to the language your child is using it is important (at some point – *not during the upset moment*) to communicate why the use of that language is problematic for getting her needs met. You may then (when she is in a calm state) model the language she needs to use in order to get her needs met. You may need to do this one thousand times before your child gets it!

Throughout the process, acknowledge that, when your child speaks to you this way, she is letting you know about feelings of distress, and that you are right there with her. Let her know that you are interested in helping her work through this feeling. If you are tired and hungry yourself, make sure you grab a snack to give yourself the energy to deal with this challenge. Remember not to take what she says personally. This is about her distress, not your inadequacy.

Scenario M: Your child gets angry and kicks a hole in the wall. What do you do?

Possible cause: He may be experiencing an overwhelming feeling of anger and probably lacks impulse control. He may be copying behavior that was observed sometime in the past, or he may simply be seeking attention.

Suggested intervention: Stay calm. Assume that he is not thinking clearly and is just feeling rageful. Remember that you should not feed the energy of the rage.

Depending on the age, size, and strength of your child, find a safe way to contain his physical aggression. With a small child, he could be safely held. With a larger, stronger child he might have to be contained in one part of the house. Unless he is physically dangerous to you, he should not be left alone after such an outburst. If he does need to be left alone, then stay in close proximity so you can monitor his behavior. Call the police or another adult for help if the situation becomes too dangerous.

Once the rage has passed and your child is thinking clearly again, talk about what happened and discuss other ways to express big, angry feelings. You might begin by having the child describe what led up to this and help the child describe "what happened." Through this discussion you can help your child describe the feelings that led to the outburst (or you can do that for the child since the child may not actually know what he or she was feeling). By accepting the feelings and helping the child put those into words, you are giving the child an alternative to showing you feelings. Then you can discuss a better way to express his feelings next time. For example, "So, it might work better if you say, "Mom, I'm really angry at you because _____."

Then you can say, "I'm so glad you told me, I know this is hard for you." Then have the child practice this a couple of times so that he is more likely to remember and use it the next time. Avoid using humiliation as a tool to motivate behavior or to "get back" at your child for damaging your home. This is a great opportunity to provide a "teachable moment," in which the natural consequence is that the child uses his allowance to purchase supplies to make home repairs and the parent helps the child make things whole again.

Scenario N: Your child is riding her bike without holding onto the handle bars, and crashes into another child. What do you do?

Possible cause: She could be practicing a new skill, showing off her new skill, or taking a risk with a skill she does not possess.

Suggested intervention: Hopefully, your child was wearing a helmet. Immediately assess the medical condition of both children as quickly as possible and seek medical help if necessary. Provide comfort to both children. If neither child is seriously injured, it is best to encourage your child to apologize to the child who was injured on the spot. Privately, discuss the incident with your child to make sure she understands why her behavior caused the accident. Restriction of the bike for a short period of time is warranted, and restriction for a longer period of time should be considered if she again exhibits similar behavior. It is important to explain that this is not intended as a punishment, but rather a necessary response to keep her safe, as a good parent keeps his child and others safe. Because she does not seem able to safely handle the bike just yet, you are going to wait until she shows that she is better able to handle it. She can do that by demonstrating improved coordination, better judgment, and an ability to put on the "brakes" in other situations when she is active and excited. Depending on the age of your child, riding a bicycle without holding onto handle bars is seen as a skill. Riding like this while wearing a helmet, and in an area where no other people or animals are around, may be acceptable depending on your personal tolerance for this normal child behavior. Most children will feel bad about hurting another person or animal, so make sure you provide emotional support to your child and let her know that accidents happen.

Scenario O: Your adolescent is supposed to be home at 9:00 p.m., but doesn't come home until midnight. What do you do?

Possible cause: Rebellion, having fun, and/or disregarding parental rules.

Suggested intervention: Provide natural consequences—do not let him go out the next time he asks. Tighten restrictions until you feel he has earned back your trust. You might say, "I'm so sorry you chose to disregard the house rules. Thank you for letting me know that I gave you more freedom than you can manage. Before you will be able to go out again in the evening, you will need to show me that you are able to manage that much freedom." Do not allow him to go out in the evening until he has demonstrated that he can act responsibly.

Scenario P: Your child does her chores as requested, but does a sloppy job. What do you do?

Possible cause: Children with low-self esteem often do things poorly, verifying for themselves that they are "worthless." Some children see their parents' expectations as unrealistically high, so they don't even try. Sometimes they do these things to engage parents in power struggles.

Suggested intervention: It is important to have small chores in the beginning, and to teach your child how to do them well. If you are consistent in your teaching, your child will eventually feel some pride in having accomplished her tasks. Sit nearby and offer verbal encouragement. Divide chores into reasonable portions. For example, instead of saying, "Please clean up your room" you might have your child start by making the bed. Then, after praising her for her efforts you could say, "Now, how about putting all the books on the shelf?" Continue in this manner until the entire task is completed.

If your child refuses to respond to your efforts, accept her refusal for the time being. When she asks you for something later, you can then ask if her chore is done. If not, let her know (calmly) that, as soon as she finishes her chore correctly, you will be happy to respond to her request. Children will often escalate and go into extreme tantrums over this, but it is important to stay calm and focused. Consider what it is you need done, and make sure to stay focused on your request, not on your child's misbehavior.

Scenario Q: Your child continually pulls your dog's tail. What do you do?

Possible cause: Your child may have been the victim of physical abuse, and is hurting the dog because he has been hurt. He may also be expressing his anger toward you or other family members by hurting something you love. He may simply lack experience with animals. Children who have experienced trauma during their development may display delays in certain areas of functioning, such as cause-and-effect thinking. Such children, who have not had sufficient experiences with receiving empathy, will have difficulty demonstrating empathy to others.

Suggested intervention: Stay calm and do not react angrily. Ask him how he is feeling. If he is angry with the dog, or with someone in the family, help him to problem-solve the situation. How can he better express his anger? If he lacks experience with animals, show him how to interact with the dog. Let him know how the dog likes to be touched and demonstrate. Practice this several times.

Scenario R: Your child does very inappropriate things in public (e.g., burping, farting). What do you do?

Possible causes:

Shame: Your child may feel that she is bad and unlovable, so she is acting in a manner consistent with her view of herself. She then acts in a way to get you to treat her in a manner congruent with her self-image. She believes that she is a "bad kid" and so she acts in a manner to get you to treat her as if she is "bad," with anger and punishment.

Lack of socialization: Past neglect may have caused your child to be ignorant of acceptable standards of conduct. She may have lacked a loving parent to help her learn social graces.

Developmental delay: Your child's early maltreatment has probably caused her to function developmentally younger than her chronological age, and she is acting accordingly.

Attention: Your child may be acting this way to get your undivided attention. Remember that children who don't know how to get positive attention will seek negative attention.

Suggested intervention: If your child is developmentally at preschool age, start with a teaching approach. Be very careful not to become angry or punitive. Do not act as if your child is bad, disgusting, or repulsive. Try hugging her and providing her with more attention and "time-in," so that she feels your love despite her behavior. Show your child that you love her and find her unconditionally accepted and valued.

Scenario S: Your child does very inappropriate things when your other children have friends over (e.g., sexual acting out). What do you do?

Possible cause: Your child may have been sexually abused in a previous home, and the visit may have triggered a trauma response. He may be experiencing anger and frustration because he does not have a friend for himself, and may be jealous of his siblings who do have friends. He may lack social skills and may fear that he will not be accepted, so he engages in behavior which is certain to keep people at a distance.

Suggested Intervention: Take your child aside and let him know that this behavior is not appropriate. Avoid shaming him. Let him know that his behavior is showing you that he needs more one-to-one time with you, and try to engage him in an activity that you will both enjoy. Be very vigilant with a child who acts out sexually— provide direct supervision (within three feet) for the duration of the visit. Work with your child's therapist to further address this issue.

Scenario T: Your child swears. What do you do?

Possible cause: Most likely, this is attention-seeking behavior. She may also be copying the behavior of her peers.

Suggested Intervention: In a calm, non-judgmental way, ask your child where she heard these words. Does she know what they mean? Children often observe that certain words result in attention from others. Let her know that this is not acceptable language in your home because your home is a safe and respectful place. Explore what words she might use when she wishes to express certain emotions (e.g. anger) toward others.

Scenario U: You tell your child that he cannot go out and play, and he takes a swing at you. What do you do?

Possible cause: Your child does not like to be told "no" and has limited or no impulse control when it comes to dealing with anger. He may have been feeling angry anyway, and your refusal to grant his request gave him a target for his anger. He may not know how to use words to express anger.

Suggested intervention: The intervention will be based on the child's developmental age, size, and physical strength. In general, when telling the child that he cannot go out and play, also tell him when he *can* go out and play—this can often diffuse his frustration before he escalates. A small child could be held on your lap while you empathize with his strong feelings and, when he's calm, explain that there are better ways for him to express his anger (give him some better ideas). An older child might be required to sit quietly, in the same room as you, for a "cooling off" period until he is ready to talk about his feelings and behavior (do not talk to/lecture him). If you send him to another room, you are reinforcing to him that you do not want to be around him. If the situation escalates to the point where either one of you is in danger, call another adult to help contain your child safely until he can calm down.

Scenario V: Your child refuses to eat dinner. What do you do?

Possible cause: Your child may not be hungry, or may refuse to eat because she is angry with you and is rejecting what you are offering. Food may have been withheld for punishment in the past, or she may have lacked adequate nutrition, so this may be an emotionally-laden issue for your child. She may simply dislike the food being served. Some children resist food (the most powerful symbol of nurturance) as a defense against their need for nurturance. When parents get into power struggles around food, they might send messages perceived as controlling and coercive by the child.

Suggested Intervention: Avoid power struggles at all costs. There are three things you cannot make a child do: eat, sleep, or use the toilet. In this case, ask your child about her feelings: is she angry about something? Tired? Sad? Let her know that, in your house, healthy snacks are always available, but the next full meal will be breakfast. Try to always include one item with dinner that your child likes (for example, applesauce).

Scenario W: Your child is obnoxious at dinner, chewing with his mouth open, etc. What do you do?

Possible cause: Food issues are so common with children who have experienced great trauma. They need to control what goes in and what comes out. Children who cannot handle any kind of intimacy frequently cannot deal with the closeness of sharing a family meal, and they attempt to spoil the meal for everyone.

Suggested Intervention: First of all, respectfully ask your child to stop this behavior. If he continues, move on to the next step. You can keep a smaller table next to the dinner table. If your child is unable to eat in an acceptable way, he can move to the other table. Avoid judgment or criticism, just let him know that this type of behavior is interfering with others enjoying their meal. If the behavior continues, you might assume that he is not hungry and excuse him from the table. If a tantrum ensues, one parent may accompany the child to his room until the family has completed their dinner.

Scenario X: Your child refuses to respond to you with anything more than one word or two. When you ask her how her day went, she says, “Fine.” When you ask what she did, she says, “Stuff.” What do you do?

Possible cause: Normal development! Children in elementary school and those who are older usually do not like to be questioned.

Suggested Intervention: Model the behavior you want by telling your child about your day. She may then respond with information about her day. Even if she doesn’t, you are demonstrating the behavior you would like to see in your child. You might also “prime the pump” so to speak, by asking about specific things (e.g., best thing, funniest thing, most frustrating thing that happened today).

Scenario Y: Your child responds, “OK, Mom” to instructions, but does so with a sarcastic attitude. What do you do?

Possible cause: He does not like to be told what to do, so he responds with anger.

Suggested intervention: Ignore the tone and focus on your child’s behavior. If he is cooperating with your directive, you may choose not to respond to the sarcasm.

Scenario Z: Your child urinates/defecates in inappropriate places in the house. What do you do?

Possible cause: This behavior may be the result of anger expressed indirectly. It may also signal a medical problem requiring evaluation by a physician. It may be fear, especially if this only happens at night—some children have been severely reprimanded and threatened if they left their beds at night and many have been molested at night. A psychotherapist or child psychiatrist should see your child to help discern the cause of this behavior and to formulate a treatment plan..

Suggested Intervention: Stay calm, don't personalize the behavior. Breathe (not deeply if it is stinky!). Have your child evaluated by a pediatrician and a psychotherapist or child psychiatrist. Chart the behavior and look for patterns or triggers. Talk calmly to your child about her behavior to assess how she expresses her understanding of the behavior. Depending on the child's age, have her help clean up. Be careful not to use humiliation as a motivator; it is sure to backfire. Keep effective cleaning solutions and rubber gloves in the home to reduce stress on the family unit. If the problem only occurs at night, it may be that the child is too fearful to go to the bathroom alone. Using nightlights and/or providing a "bed pan/bucket" nearby might help.

CHAPTER 5

Adjusting Expectations

It is clear that parenting children who have disorders of attachment takes a Herculean amount of energy, strength, dedication, patience and perseverance. It takes redefining the notion of success, both yours as a parent and the child's as a functioning member of society. It means grieving unfulfilled dreams. It also means that you cannot give so much of yourself during the process that both you, your child, and your family ultimately lose. One key to successfully parenting children with disorders of attachment is adjusting expectations.

Taking care of yourself

When families finally find their way to ATTACh, they have usually spent years trying to get help for their child. Most of these weary parents have suffered years of isolation from family and friends, accusations of bad parenting and, for some, abuse at the hands of their children. It is important that parents remember that they cannot help their child heal until they help themselves.

You may be "crazy" now, but you didn't necessarily start out that way

To quote Dr. Gregory Keck, parents often say something similar to, "I don't really **want** to count all the cookies in the cookie jar." The lying and manipulative behavior often seen in children with disorders of attachment leads parents to do things that would appear "crazy" to outsiders. In addition, parents often become so attuned to their children's moods and behaviors that they can predict how their children will react to certain triggers. The anticipation of these "reactions" can cause extreme anxiety in the caregiver. Parents do feel crazy after living 24/7 with these children—it would be highly irregular if they did not. Once feeling this way, however, the question is what can be done to bring normalcy back to the home?

The old adage, "the parent must get better before the child can get better," is especially true for the main caregiver of children with disorders of attachment. Along with trying to tame an unruly child, the main caregiver is usually also dealing with the loss of dreams and expectations of parenting. Lack of sleep and constant vigilance, coupled with this grief, often leads to clinical depression or post-traumatic stress disorder. Caregivers who are feeling totally overwhelmed, disillusioned and without hope need to see a doctor for an evaluation for depression and anxiety. These are normal reactions to very abnormal life experiences, and luckily very treatable! If treatment is recommended, parents need to give themselves permission to receive that help. Depression is not a sign of weakness. On the contrary, seeking help is a sign of strength. Healing yourself is the first step toward the healing of your child.

When you are the parent of a two-year-old child you are always watchful for what the child will do or get into that may be harmful. Following a two-year-old around for any length of time can be tiresome, but at least a parent can put things up out of reach or take other precautions to keep their child, and others in the home, safe. In contrast, the parents of a child with disorders of attachment are "on alert" at all times, as if they were parenting a young child but without the ability to take precautions. This constant, unrelenting state of vigilance is exhausting for caregivers, making time away essential for the well-being of the parent. Respite care is available in some areas for families who need time away from their child, but it may take some research to find it. A good place to start is adopting.org, which has a list of respite organizations by state. Local therapists or county mental health offices may also be helpful in locating these services. If professional respite care is unavailable, using family members or someone from the community, local church or temple can be an option.

It is imperative for caregivers to have this time to rejuvenate. In many cases the children misbehave more after respite, making the parent feel that they are better off simply staying home with their children. When they do not take time away from the child, however, parents feel even more isolated and begin to feel as if they are prisoners in their own home. This can result in broken marriages and increased loss for all children in the home. Regardless of the child's reaction to time away from the caregiver, parents must have time alone, time to spend together as a couple, and time to spend as a family.

Parents will find that it is difficult to confide in their friends or family regarding their challenges with their children. Parenting a child with disorders of attachment is very different from parenting a child with normal emotional development. Trying to confide in people who do not understand can lead to increased frustration on the part of the caregiver and lead to feelings of hopelessness. It is vitally important for the caregiver to network with others who are raising children with these disorders through support groups, attendance at conferences, listservs and personal communication. The ability to be understood and not judged is reaffirming for the caregiver, and continual support is necessary for successful parenting.

At times, support through networking is not enough to help caregivers with the pain, grief, loss, and hopelessness they feel. Speaking to someone about the guilt felt over not being able to feel love for your child is not a subject one would bring up in casual conversation. As the child needs therapy to deal with his or her difficulties, so does a caregiver. Being able to talk to an objective listener helps parents face their past, deal with their present and make plans for their future. This support can be sought through a therapeutic setting, with a member of the clergy or through other community services. Many Christian churches have Stephen Ministers who help parishioners at no cost.

However parents seek help, whether it is through diagnosis and treatment of depression and anxiety, respite, and/or therapeutic help, support for caregivers plays a vital role in the healing process.

Every day life is no longer "every day life"

Being a parent is one of the most difficult jobs in the world. Living with and parenting a child who has a disorder of attachment is far more challenging and impossible to describe. One has to "live it" to fully understand the complexities of every day life.

Life with a child who has a disorder of attachment is all consuming. Gone is the social life you once knew. Even the simplest things in life, like going to the grocery store, become difficult. Holidays bring a sense of dread rather than happiness. Going out in public often over-stimulates the child, bringing on negative behaviors, which can be embarrassing at best and a safety issue at worst. As a result, some families rarely leave the house with their child and become isolated from friends and co-workers. Attendance at family gatherings often diminishes as well, further isolating the caregivers.

It is hard to continue relationships with family and friends once you are parenting a child who has a disorder of attachment. The need for a different kind of parenting is not recognized by most people who do not understand the reasoning behind, and benefits of, therapeutic parenting. People "looking in" see a child without scars and who looks "healthy." The damage to the brain, in most cases, has not affected the child's cognitive abilities, so the damage to the areas controlling emotion are not obvious to those outside the home. Since they do not "see" anything wrong with the child they tend to blame the parents for the behaviors they see. Unfortunately, this does not only happen with family members and friends, but also occurs in the professional realm. School personnel, child welfare case workers, therapists and those working in the judicial system often judge families inappropriately, due to their lack of understanding and knowledge of this disorder. It is hard enough to deal with the bureaucracy of the mental health system. When current parents are blamed for the results of abandonment, abuse or neglect in early childhood or deemed to be "bad parents" it is disheartening and can add to a parent's sense of despair.

Within the home parents must also be very wary of the child's ability to triangulate them. These children are masters at pushing buttons parents did not even know they had, and the main caretaker is usually the parent who is targeted the most. When the father comes home it is not uncommon for the child to push mom's last button, sending her over the edge just as dad walks in the door. Dad then sees an angelic child and a mother who is out of control. At that point it is the dad's job to support the mother and let the child know this behavior will not be tolerated. Parents must be united. When a child is allowed to divide the parents, the family won't survive in a healthy way.

When dreams collide with reality

Sometimes taking care of yourself means grieving for unfulfilled dreams. Most parents were relatively happy before their children came into their care. Many were even anxiously waiting for the day when their children would arrive and they could become the happy family they had always dreamed of being. Unfortunately real life rarely lives up to the dream.

"Loving" a child who can't attach in healthy ways has an entirely different meaning, which will never be found in Webster's Dictionary. Most parents and their children bond while the child is an infant. The gaze and interaction between the parent and child, as well as the comfort and touch provided, creates a loving, safe environment for both. How do you "love" a child whose gaze seems always filled with hate? Whose embrace appears meant to hurt? Whose mission in life seems to make you feel as miserable as he or she feels inside?

If our children could feel safe enough to accept love, their world and ours would be a much better place. Until that acceptance is possible, caretakers need to change their expectations of how they should "feel" about the child. It is impossible to "love" someone who does not reciprocate that love. As parents of children with disorders of attachment we have to learn to love a different way. This may entail giving up some of the original "dream" we had before our children arrived. For many, especially mothers, it also means letting go of the guilt we harbor for not feeling the way a mother "should" about her child and also letting go of the anger over lost dreams. Letting go of the anger and guilt will help a parent begin to dream again, this time a more realistic dream.

The new dream will entail a child who can feel a bit of empathy for others, a young adult who has graduated from high school without spending time in juvenile hall, an adult who can hold a job and is not addicted to alcohol or drugs. Realistic dreams must be attainable. Sometimes those dreams consist solely of keeping our children safe, off the streets and out of jail...for as long as we can.

How do we attain those dreams? It is not easy and there is no quick fix, no magic pill. We learn to "love" our children our way by keeping them and other members of the family safe. We spend hours driving to and from therapy. We "love" them by adding structure to their day, by staying attuned to their moods and needs and by changing the way we parent. We "love" them by giving up our need to "control" all aspects of their world, giving them acceptable choices whenever possible and allowing natural consequences to take care of bad choices. We "love" them by learning to respond without anger, condemnation or despair, but with a calm, empathetic appreciation and understanding of their pain and their fear. We "love" them our way and continue to pray for the day they will begin to return that love in any way they can.

Redefining success

Consider the following story from an adoptive mom:

Jenna is almost 21 years old. Today is the seventh anniversary of her adoption. When she first came home, she used to say she wanted to be a veterinarian when she grew up. It did not seem out of the question based on her love of animals, intelligence and diligence the first year she was home.

All that quickly fell apart her freshman year in high school and it took four years of fighting, restricting, monitoring, supervising and structuring for her to even graduate from high school. A year has passed since graduation and she will be 21 in the fall. This last year has been the year from hell.

After graduation, she immediately challenged all rules and "ran away" on several occasions. Her first "foray" into independence and living on her own, she plummeted within a week beginning with a drunk driving accident and ending with getting fired from her job and kicked out of her apartment. Without the "external structure" of our home, rules and routine, she was unable to function and had no choice but to come home.

She beat us up constantly with her rage, resentment, and the magnitude of her dependence upon us. After several false starts, and enduring her rage at us when she was forced by circumstances to return home, we finally asked her to leave because of the toll it was taking on our family. She had a brief period of doing well, securing an outstanding job and even earning "Employee of the Month." After several incidents of coming to work late, she sealed her fate in response to being "warned" by her bosses that she needed to reflect commitment to her job through being on time. The very next day she came in one hour late.

A few months passed during which she essentially went on "vacation," securing a marginal part-time job, playing a lot, and not being in a big hurry to get a job that would cover her bills. She owes her roommates for three month's rent, has maxed out every credit card she so eagerly applied for to "build up her credit score," has not paid us her very low car payment (she couldn't qualify for a loan so we bought a car out-of-pocket) for three months. She even enrolled in college and dropped out in a single day, but neglected to tell the school or withdraw formally. She now owes the university hundreds of dollars.

Her ability to manage the responsibilities of daily life is nil. She lives for the "pleasure principle"—if it is fun, do it; if it isn't, who cares? A natural and logical consequence of failure to pay us her car payment would be to take the car away, but that would only make her more dependent upon us and limit her options for employment.

We feel trapped by her dysfunction, yet have begun to slowly identify areas where we will no longer assist her. We will not pay her bad debts. We will not cover her expenses to live independently, but have offered that she can come home if she needs to. She refuses, saying she wants her freedom, but it is her freedom that she cannot handle. We took her off our car insurance and signed the title of the car over to her so that another accident would not impact our family and our other children. We also wanted to be sure that we could not be sued for any irresponsibility, careless-

ness, or recklessness. She is uncovered by our insurance. Since she is no longer a student, she has no insurance coverage of her own.

We have spent thousands of dollars on psychiatric care and medication out-of-pocket, only to have her discontinue the meds because she doesn't feel like taking them anymore. We have given her the numbers for public assistance and the community care clinics. We have resigned ourselves to the fact this may be her life—debt, barely getting by, multiple jobs, self-sabotage and low-income living. It is not what we had hoped for her, but it may be as good as it gets.

This heart-wrenching story is not an uncommon one. No matter how hard you try, how much money you spend, or how many different interventions you use, some children simply cannot overcome their dysfunction to become what we would typically consider a loving family member and contributing member of society.

This does not mean you have failed. You have succeeded in giving your child a chance to overcome childhood trauma and heal. You have utilized all of the resources at your disposal to try to help her. You have given her the experience of being loved and cared for and experiencing "normal" family life. You have sacrificed a great deal. You have endured a lot of abuse. You have done what most people would not—you tried. And who knows—the seeds that you have planted may take a stronger hold as your child matures, and she may improve in time.

Also, this does not mean your child has failed. For some children, simply being able to exist outside of an institutional setting is a success. For others, keeping suicidal thoughts at bay is a success. It's all a matter of perspective. Try to focus on how far your child has come, rather than how far she has yet to go.

Grieving unfulfilled dreams

Most parents harbor hopes and dreams for the adults their children will become and the futures they will have. Often, children who have disorders of attachment do not come close to fulfilling these dreams. The grief that results from this is real, and many parents need professional help to come to terms with it.

Following are two such stories:

As a mom I never had any preconceived notions or expectations of what I wanted my children to "be" when they grew up. My only desire was that they would be productive citizens with good character and enjoy whatever vocation they chose. My greatest sorrow and sense of loss and disappointment has been in her character and values, or lack thereof, not in what my daughter has chosen to do as a vocation.

Our daughter is almost 21 and stunningly beautiful. She is funny, gregarious, engaging and intelligent. Upon first glance, most people are completely taken by her. Underneath all those external attributes is a young woman who is careless, irresponsible, disregarding, occasionally cruel, manipulative, controlling, defiant, and a con. She lives to defy and defeat the efforts of others on her behalf, and thoroughly enjoys the power she wields in playing with, toying with, and outsmarting her victims. Sadly, her "victims" are anyone who cares enough about her to want to be involved with her or help her. She lies as easily as she breathes and rarely tells the truth. She likes to play both ends against the middle and works hard at divide and conquer. She would draw you in with her vulnerability and "I need you" sweetness, only to turn and reject you after you responded to her cry for help. It was like she had an "evil twin."

It took me a whole year of conflict and sorrow to recognize that she was an empty shell who "crafted" a new her to fit each occasion, and she was not the young girl with potential that I needed her to be. It was difficult to learn to parent her from the perspective of, "I can never trust her" vs. the perspective of, "how can she earn our trust?" I didn't think I was a big enough person to be able to love someone I couldn't even like. After a full year of grieving, including some time when I could not be around her, I have finally found that place where I can—with great effort—love her despite her character flaws. I have learned to live with the fact that I have a daughter who is a liar and a con. ***The biggest loss has been that this is not the type of mother I imagined I would to be.***

Another story:

There I was, thinking I would have and live the American Dream, or at least my dream. I had it all planned out. At 26 I would get married, be a good wife, and from a loving marriage we would have six beautiful children. I would work, but spend an enormous amount of time loving and admiring my six wonderful children. Oh, life would be so grand as I would be sure to show each of my children how I cherished the day they were born.

Well, things never went quite the way I had planned. It seemed that God had another plan for me. I am a single mom with two children who have disorders of attachment. Let me tell you, it takes a very extraordinary and courageous person to raise children with special needs. I thought I would be married with six children. Here I am a lesbian with not one, but two, girls who have disorders of attachment.

I know you're thinking, "Didn't she get it the first time? Why would she take a second chance?" I often ask myself that very question, but at the time I thought these children would not make it in any other home. My feeling was that they would have gone from house to house, never having a home. Well, they finally have a home, which for me sometimes feels liked a battle field. There have been long periods where day-to-day life has been a constant struggle. Let me give you a little insight on the past eight years.

My first is now 16 yrs old. She has been in 11 homes, counting that of her biological mother, and has been adopted once with her biological brother. Needless to say, she came with a lot of anger and hurt. I adopted her in 1999, and since I was working at an attachment center, I felt I could handle the responsibility. Well, I had no idea what it was like to raise a child, especially one with a disorder of attachment.

She came in ready to show me how I could not keep her safe and how she had a damaged heart. These are two things she let me know up front. I should have taken her words wisely, because for the next 6 years she was determined to keep these statements true. She was so afraid to let go and be loved. She would steal on a regular basis and lie daily. For instance, one time the teacher at school let me know how I was not taking good care of her, because she needed a pair of glasses. She had convinced the teacher that I had not responded to her needs. Oh, yes, the attention she got from the doctor was just the beginning. I'm sure you already know the length of time it took to get her glasses and, of course, there was extra attention because she is such a "beautiful well mannered child." We even got two pair for the price of one. The next day she went to school with the ones I had chosen and, wouldn't you know it, some kid asked a question or made a negative statement about her glasses. That was all she needed. When they went on a field trip far away from home, she decided to throw her new glasses away. I got so many stories: the wind blew them off her head; someone accidentally knocked them off; she just couldn't find them. I'm sure you know where I'm going with this. Of course, the truth was never told. This is the thick of it; she begins to cry and tells me, "See, this is why I don't tell you things, you never believe me. I am trying to tell you the truth, but you won't listen." So, I say to her, "Which story would like for me to believe?" and she gets quiet and says, "Oh yeah" and walks away. So I think to myself, "Now how did this get turned on me…?"

Welcome to being a mother with a child who has a disorder of attachment. You become the crazy one. She went further to let me know that, "Maybe someday I will let you be my mom." I finally got what she was telling me about a year into it. The first year was very difficult. I couldn't find the therapist I needed and people couldn't support me because they had no idea what I was talking about. I began to feel unfit as a parent, and that I just couldn't get it right. I did not have a support system and people believed her, not me. What I mean is, I believe they did not suspect she had a disorder of attachment; they simply thought that I could not care for her. I was often reminded that it was because I was a new parent, I did not understand her and I should be easier on her. I was even called Bipolar by one of my best friends. I was told she was such a pretty girl and she could not be as bad as I was saying. I was constantly questioned and taken out of my role as her parent.

Despite all of the progress she has made, she still struggles with relationships, mostly with boyfriends, but the issues are now more manageable and "normal." She was one of the fortunate ones. She came with a social worker who understood her issues. She and I were sent to an attachment center where we learned skills and tools to deal with her issues. After six years of good therapy, support from family and friends and lots and lots of good fun trips and outings with friends, I survived. She is now going to the 12th grade, with hopes of graduating and earning a volleyball scholarship. She has never been pregnant, on drugs or gone to jail. She has hopes and dreams. She has friendships and someday wants to be a parent and a wife. I now believe she will achieve her goals. She will still call on me, probably more than the average child, but it looks like she will make it or at least will have a fighting chance. And I can safely say she is attached and accepts me as her mother, but it took six of the seven years.

My second child is was born in China and adopted by a family at 2 ½ yrs old. The family was warned that she was the "worst" and was urged to consider another child who might better suit their family. The family chose her regardless of the warning. They took her home an attempted to nurture and care for her, but felt her behaviors were unmanageable.

She has been in five homes counting her biological family. Families have met with her anger toward younger children, afraid that she might hurt or even kill them. Coming into my home there were no younger children. However, when younger children were around she was competitive, but never showed signs of wanting to hurt anyone, except for me, of course. It seemed that her anger was getting progressively worse, and there was one day I was more convinced than ever that her mission was to hurt me. As we sat in the car one evening, I began to have a conversation with her. I let her know that I knew what her intent was and that it was to hurt me. I shared with her that if she did, I knew where I was going because I had been a good person and heaven is where I would end up. Not because she hurt me, but because it would simply be my time to go. As I spoke, tears formed in her eyes and began to overflow. Then I asked her, "Where would you go if you hurt me?" I asked her again to think about where she would go. She began to cry even harder. My oldest had warned me that she was afraid her sister would try to hurt or kill me once she got older. I was never really afraid, but she didn't know that. I felt, and still feel, that she has had this myth come true in her mind. She has been asked to leave other homes because they were fearful she would harm their younger children. I do believe she is attempting to make this happen in my head as well.

We also fostered a younger boy and she would talk of killing him. I asked her to write out her plan. Once I read it, it was clear she really did not have one. I can't say that her anger will not get worse or that she won't try to hurt me, but I don't live my life around it either. She, unlike her sister, has not bought into therapy or family. She truly believes she has no need for adults in her life except for a roof over her head and food on the table. Otherwise, she believes she can take care of herself. Despite her anger, she has some good goals and plans to become a pediatrician as well as buy a big house. I believe she will achieve these goals, but possibly live by herself with some chosen animals. Academically she does well. She is very driven! She knows how to achieve her goals through money and power. She is in one of the best private schools on scholarship. She makes honor roll and is on her way to the 7th grade. When she entered our home, she could not read or write. She had been held back in Kindergarten and was on her way to the 2nd grade. It has been six long years and she has not attached, but her behaviors are more manageable most of the time. She has friends, but they do most of the work. Even if they call and leave a message, she is afraid to call back out of fear that they will not be available.

As a parent of these children you live in your own home feeling like the enemy. It makes it difficult to have intimate relationships, because you are tired, angry and hurt. You are always scared to let your guard down because you never know when they (children with disorders of attachment) will attack. People don't want to acknowledge that something may be wrong with your child(ren), because then they may have to take a look at themselves or support what you see and then they might feel helpless and/or hopeless too. So they tune out and act as if it doesn't exist, blaming you. If we look unhappy then we are labeled the mean, selfish parent. "By God that child needs us!" Then we question our own self worth.

People have asked would I do it again if I had the chance. Although I don't regret having my two girls come into my life, I could honestly say without a doubt I would never do this again. It takes a lot of work to manage these children. It very rarely feels like a family. My house often feels like a treatment facility. If I could get paid for all the hours I have put in, I would probably be a millionaire by now. I have been made to feel like an outcast in my home and community. Although my family is supportive for the most part, there were and still are times I am questioned about my parenting style. Oh yeah, regular parenting does not work with these children. People just don't understand what you are going through.

The journey is the destination

Following is another adoptive mom's story:

When you become a parent, you do not know what lies ahead for you. You are thrilled to hold your new baby no matter from whence he came. You want the best for him. You want him to be happy. You are convinced that his life will be a good one because you love him with all your heart. You want to be a good parent. You read, you sing, you teach, you hope. In your child's journey, you meet people who want for him what you want as a parent…teachers, coaches, principals, friends. You and they want your child to be successful and feel happy.

Your child grows older. You start feeling like your child is different; you are anxious because he is not making friends. You are told he is not developing as he should. Your child gets into trouble. You are told that he is acting badly and misbehaving. You have loved him with all your might. You feel terrible. You feel ashamed. You feel guilty. You feel angry. You feel overwhelming sadness. You worry. You begin to doubt many things about yourself and your parenting. Everyone has easy advice to give for "fixing" your child and the family situation. You talk to professionals. You read book after book. You pray that this time the advice will work. Once again you feel hopeful. Things get better. Life gets easier. Then…the cycle begins again. The journey continues."

I recently wrote the previous journal entry shortly after I withdrew our 12-year-old son from 7th grade and his middle school. On the one hand, it was not an easy decision since the alternative meant home schooling him for the remainder of the school year. On the other hand, the decision was a simple one since he was so unhappy at this school and felt like a failure. It was simply not working.

Within the first week of being home, he began to come back. He started reading again, he was more physically active and he was happier. I learned from this experience to trust my instincts. As a parent, with a child like mine, I am put often into situations where I need to assess whether things are working for him or not. I have also learned that there are people with whom my child will spend time who "get" him and many more who don't. Those who don't understand him feed into my doubts, my worries, and my confidence in parenting. Those who do "get" him offer support, encouragement, and build his self-esteem.

One of my jobs as a parent is to help him stay strong and confident no matter with whom he spends his time. When my son was younger, I felt badly that he wasn't like the other kids. He couldn't play on a soccer team. He couldn't go on a play date. He couldn't control his frustration. He couldn't go out to a restaurant. After struggling with this over and over, I learned what he *could* do and helped him find those things instead. He could put almost anything together by himself. He could remember lyrics to songs after hearing them once. He could create a story and tell it. He could cook his own food. He could read an entire novel in a day. He could make us laugh.

As a parent, this is what we must do. We find the many things our children feel successful doing and we make sure they have the opportunity to do these. Recently, my son came home from camp wearing a T-shirt that read, "The journey is the destination." I realized that, once again, this is the child I have been given, and every step of the way, whether easy or difficult, is part of the journey and for that, I am thankful.

CHAPTER 6

Loss: The Hidden Trauma

As if the issues that children who have disorders of attachment bring to the family aren't enough, parents often have their own unresolved issues, which are barriers to attachment.

Loss and adoption

It has been hypothesized that all those who come to adoption do so because of a loss. Children who have been adopted have lost their birth families. Birth families have lost their children. However, there is not a great deal of information about the losses experienced by those who choose to adopt. Rather, it is assumed that because adoptive parents fulfill their dream of creating a family, their experience is all positive and full of good things.

In reality, most—if not all—adoptive parents come to adoption because of a loss they have experienced. The most common loss associated with adoption is infertility. Those experiencing infertility have usually exhausted a large portion of their financial and emotional resources in their effort to conceive a child. This process can be painful, exhausting, and emotionally draining. People also acknowledge experiencing a sense of shame. Conceiving a child is presumed to be a natural biological function; being unable to create a family in this way leads to a myriad of emotions. Since procreation is a natural process, there is a sense that someone must be to blame if a child is not produced. By the same token, everyone has an opinion about why conception might not be taking place. Although people may be well-meaning in their concern, their comments tend to add to the sense of guilt, shame, and loss that the overwhelmed, emotionally depleted, prospective parents are experiencing.

Parents who are unable to conceive a child biologically will often turn to adoption as an alternative way to build a family. However, by the time they make this decision, they have sometimes come to it out of a sense of desperation, believing that there is no other way to have a family. They often transfer the dream they had of a birth child onto the child they hope to adopt. Since most families are interested in having children as young as possible and who resemble them in some way, they tend to have those children in mind when they begin to consider adoption. Unconsciously, adoptive parents sometimes believe that the child they are adopting will be similar to the child they have been unable to create biologically.

As prospective adoptive parents begin the home study process, they are asked to identify why they have chosen adoption. If the answer to the question is infertility, they are often asked how they have resolved this issue. Because infertility is a loss, it is experienced in the same way as death, divorce, or any other type of loss. It is a process that impacts people at various times during their lives. Infertility is something that is integrated into other life experiences; it is not ever really resolved. So, for a woman who is infertile, it can be very challenging when her adolescent daughter who is adopted becomes sexually active. Being unable to conceive herself, this mother is frightened for all the things all mothers are. However, in addition she might feel some resentment toward her daughter because her child can possibly do something that she herself cannot. This could cause additional tension in an already stress-filled parent-child relationship.

In adoption, as in all forms of parenting, it is important that the parent gets to a point of feeling entitled to parent. All parents begin the journey feeling (to different extents) inept and insecure. In biological families, usually parents get to grow into their roles and begin to claim their power as parents. These parents are then better able to handle direct challenges to their authority as their children get older. Many children say things like “I hate you” or “I wish you weren't my parent.” While these are often hurtful statements, healthy, “entitled” parents can maintain perspective that this is really about the child's resistance to limits rather than a true evaluation of the parent. However, adoptive parents, especially those who have struggled with infertility, may feel very wounded by these comments. They may at some level doubt their right to be a parent. These insecurities may be triggered by feelings that the child is actively rejecting the parent. These insecurities can undermine the parent-child relationship at a critical time when, in the course of normal development, the child begins to push against the parent in a struggle for autonomy and independence. The child needs the parent to tolerate this struggle while still maintaining a foundation of connection to the child. If the child interprets the parent's reaction as withdrawal or insecurity, then the parent-child relationship can become submerged in greater conflict, fear, and resentment.

Not everyone who comes to adoption comes to it because of infertility. There are those who would assert that they have experienced no losses that have led them to make this life decision. There are others, however, who have come to see that they were led to this decision by their own life experiences. Some people who adopt had very unhappy childhood experiences. Consequently, they have determined that they will help another child so that this child does not need to have a similar experience. Some people who have always lived disadvantaged lives are sensitive to the plight of poor children and want to provide a better life for them. Many single parents and same-sex parents choose to adopt because they determine it is a better option for them than biological procreation.

No matter what the reason, families who adopt are building their family in a way that is not considered by most of society to be “the normal way to have children.” This perception alone can lead to a feeling of difference on the part of the adoptive family. If this is not addressed and discussed in the family, this too can lead to additional tension. Because there are so many children in need of homes, any reason potential parents have for wanting to raise a child not born to them should be respected. However, it is helpful for potential parents to be able to explore the basis for their desire to adopt with a trusted person or group during the home study process. This equips the parents with knowledge about themselves that strengthens their resolve and helps them stay centered when they are dealing with the havoc that children with disorders of attachment can cause in a home.

Other types of loss

Adoptive parents are not the only parents who have feelings of loss that impact their ability to parent. This is also true of many families who have children by birth. Mothers who suffer from post-partum depression may have great difficulty bonding with their children. These women are often expending all of their energy just trying to stay alive. As they begin to recover, these parents often feel great loss due to being unable to provide for their child as they had wished. Similarly, when children are born prematurely and spend a great deal of their early lives attached to life-supporting technology and living in an incubator, it is difficult for parents to provide as much nurturing as they would like. This leads to feelings of loss, as this is not the way that they envisioned the early months of parenting to be.

There are many other reasons why parents may feel loss regarding their parenting experience. Divorce and custody issues can impact bonding and attachment. If parents experience illness or a death shortly after the birth of a child, this can substantially impact their ability to attach to their child. Military families are another group of parents who have experienced separations that impact their relationships with their children. Although they may not have chosen the separation, these parents still experience feelings of loss and grief about having to leave their children. What is important to remember is that issues of loss and grief impact the relationships that develop between parents and children no matter how children come into a family. It is certainly more frequently noted and discussed in the area of adoption, but it is possible to have these concerns in any family.

The dream child

Before becoming parents, each of us had a dream of what our child might be like. Each of us had an idea of what type of parent we would be. Many of us were very clear that we would not parent in the same way our own parents did. By the same token, we had an idea—most likely it was unconscious—of the type of child we would have. This child can be referred to as our dream child. Maybe we thought we would have a child who resembled us in physical features. More than likely we thought we would have a child much more attractive than we are. Our child might be athletic, bright, or talented in a specific area. Most of all, we dream of children in our family who are happy, who enjoy spending time with us and who are fun to parent. We are all realistic enough to know that the child of whom we dreamed does not exist. Every human being has flaws and every relationship has its struggles. No matter how children come into a family, there can be bumps in the road as we work to get them to adulthood. We survive our negative experiences and even learn to laugh at some of the conflicts we have with our kids. We realize that not only is this child not our dream child, we are not the child's dream parents. We all adjust and move forward.

For those of us whose children have experienced severe trauma this is not the way our story is told. Very few of us dreamed of children who were developmentally delayed, who had horrific tantrums that could last for hours, who could physically harm others, and who were unable to connect to us (their parents) in any meaningful way. That was not our dream; however, for so many of us, it has become our nightmare.

Loving our children is not enough to change behaviors over which they have little or no control. As parents, we are angry that the child we wanted, dreamed of, and brought into our family, is unable to really be a part of our family. In fact, our child is often the cause of so much chaos that we begin to wonder if we even are a family any more. Most of us read a great deal. We are like sponges, taking in everything that is said to us, willing to try anything that will help our child (and our family) have a life that even resembles normal. We go to every conference; we listen to everyone who speaks on this subject. We travel for hours trying to find someone who can help us help our child. So many times, things don't improve or they improve very little. As parents we try to focus as much as we can on the needs of our child; however, this entire process is a great loss for us. We need to grieve that this experience is not what we thought was going to happen. We need to understand that grieving the experience is not a negative thing. We can love our child while grieving that things are not as we expected they would be. When children change families and lose people close to them, we know they grieve. When children in their original families have experienced a parent's depression, domestic violence, or a long separation, they need to grieve as well.

For so many of us, we began this journey by wanting to help a child in need, or simply to experience parenthood. We planned to provide so much and we had hoped to see our child grow and change. We looked forward to sharing hugs, having fun family time, and eventually, as our children reached adulthood, possibly becoming friends. For so many of our kids, this is as difficult as asking them to walk without legs. It is incredibly sad for them, but it is also sad for us. No act of love is ever wasted. As we continue to work diligently to help our children have the best experiences they can have, we also need to tend to ourselves. We need to find ways to meet our needs while still doing the best we can to take care of our children. Loss permeates the experience of adoption, kinship care, and families touched by depression, substance abuse, domestic violence, or long separations. We all feel it; we have all experienced it. It is not something that is just about our children. It is also about us. We must grieve what we thought we would have, how we pictured we would be. We need to share with one another or with a trusted friend or therapist. By so doing, we are creating a bridge that will reach others because we will not be closed and desolate. The other option is to ignore or swallow our losses, pretend everything is as it should be and use our losses to create a door that we push shut so that others can't get to us. Because of the way their life experiences have impacted their development, this is what our children have done. It is a mechanism to survive; however, we constantly see that it does not work well for them.

Albert Einstein once said, “There are two ways to live your life—one is as though nothing is a miracle, the other is as though everything is a miracle.” Looking for the miracles in our parenting (and there are many), helps us balance our losses. Realizing that we are still able to put one foot in front of the other is a miracle. Getting a hug from someone who loves us is a miracle (it doesn’t have to be our child). Once we make peace with our losses, the power of loss can be transformed into strength, giving us an opportunity to see miracles and to realize that each one of us —and our families—truly is a miracle.

CHAPTER 7

Stories from the Front Lines

A mom's story

My foster daughter is 13 now, has lived with me for a year and we've begun the adoption process. We started the year with her going into rages and four months ago she actually went after her older sister with a knife. Then she was mad that I was holding *her* responsible—after all, her sister had deserved it and therefore was to blame! Often times after the rage, she would either not remember it very well or would choose not to accept that it had happened. The scariest rages happened in the car when she would either try to hurt me while I was driving or throw herself out of the car. She was eventually able to articulate that she was scared of becoming close to me. I'm her third mother—she was adopted for ten years before coming back into the foster care system. Her adoptive parents abused her severely, to the point that the state investigator described it to the judge as deliberate physical and emotional torture.

We finally came up with a couple of strategies that helped:

- She does not call me "mom" or "mother" or anything similar. Currently she is calling me by my first name, but we're looking for something else for her to call me. This helps her separate me from her first adoptive mother and her birth mother.
- I have to remain calm through her rages. My voice actually is a bit lower and calmer when she is raging. It helps give her an "island of calm" in the storming. The counselor gave her a cognitive image of trying to "swim to the island" when she's in a rage. To get there, she has to lower her voice, begin to take deep, slow breaths and try to still her body. It took several rages, but she began to try it and it worked after about five rages or so. Not every time, but often she is able to calm herself down enough to go to a different room or go for a walk until her rage passes.
- We work on a list of acceptable words almost every day. What words should she use for different emotions and thoughts? We discovered that she had a very small emotional vocabulary outside of vulgar words. As she has built up her emotional vocabulary, her raging has become less vulgar and more colorful. In fact, I've been able to break some of her rages by repeating one of the big words she'll use for the first time and asking her what it means. It disrupts her rage, distracts her and gives her a chance to regain some space. Other times she'll mangle a word or misuse it and I'll repeat the word in a questioning voice and it will cause her to laugh. Again—disrupting the rage.
- When she does go into a rage, once she has calmed back down we agree on some consequences. However, her consequences are also tied to incentives. First, we approach it from a "love and logic" perspective—the rage exhausted me and drained all my energy. So she needs to do some of my normal tasks while I regain energy. If she does specific tasks every day for a week or two weeks, depending on the severity of the rage, then she will earn her computer time. She still has to do her normal chores to earn her computer time. Its just that the new consequences have to be done as part of the basic every day requirements for computer time to even be considered. Since she *loves* to use the computer, this has been extremely effective. What's nice is that many of those consequences have since crept into her every day interactions—checking to see if I need more water while she's going into the kitchen to get herself something, etc.

We've gone from two or three rages a day down to a very few at all. Her last major rage was seven months ago. She's come close a couple of times, then stopped herself, told me that she needed to take a walk and abruptly left the house and 30 minutes later returned. Then she will tell me that her anger was gaining the upper hand, so she had to "use her coping skills." It's amazing how she has picked up on the lingo. She's also begun to go into a rage and managed to keep it small and short. In other words, yelling and screaming, but no violence and little vulgarity (although still definitely aimed at me).

We've also worked extensively with a child psychiatrist at a major university and a Dialectical Behavioral Therapy (DBT) counselor to get this far. The medications seem to enable her to have more cognitive control and have made a real difference. If she forgets to take her mood stabilizer, then she'll probably have a lot of anger issues. She tells me that she is scared of getting too emotionally bonded to me, but that she really wants to at the same time. And slowly, she is bonding. It's an amazing change. Enough of a change that her adoptive parents agreed to voluntarily relinquish parental rights provided that I adopted her. They wanted a commitment from the children's division that they would only allow me to adopt her, no one else.

Its been a long year and we have a LOOOOOONG way to go. But she's putting everything into improving and trying to learn how to be a full, participating member of a family, something she never has had. It appears that she has not attached to anyone except her sisters before now. It's awesome to see such a cool teenager emerge from this box of rage.

A child's story

Most of my life trusting people had been the hardest thing. Growing up, I had moved around to several different foster homes and I began to believe that staying in one home would be impossible for me. I went into the foster care system at the age of two and was first adopted at the age of six. My first adoption didn't even work out therefore I had to move into a group home and then a few other foster homes.

My first adoptive home was where a lot happened that changed my life. I went into that home with my blood brother. He's six years older than me so he was twelve. The reason that we left our last home was because our foster parents wanted to adopt me without my brother. My social worker at the time told the parents that it was either both of us or neither one of us. Those parents passed up on the offer so my brother and I moved out on our way to a home that our social worker told us would be a permanent one. I remember sitting behind the driver's seat crying and holding my Barbie. My brother was behind the passenger's seat just sitting there, looking out of the car window. I honestly don't think that I really knew what was going on. It was just the simple fact that I had seen all my things being boxed up and put into the trunk and somehow I knew that feeling, it was already familiar to me and I hated it. That feeling meant moving somewhere unfamiliar, having to meet new people all over again, new house, new surroundings, new rules, new school, and the hardest: new parents.

My first adoptive home wasn't at all what a little girl thought it would be. Of course I thought that my father was a dream. He was funny and everything that he did with or for me just made me feel like he cared so much. I felt loved. This man was a single father and the only man that really felt like a dad. He became the only father that I really knew. He took care of my hair better than some of my foster mothers had. He made sure that I knew how to clean and take care of myself. I remember the first time he came into the bathroom while I was taking a bath. I felt a little weird because I knew better and men usually don't help you bathe. He made me feel comfortable and safe then he told me what I was doing wrong and right to bathe myself correctly. I didn't have night clothes so I would wear his t-shirts to bed. My brother found a friend in the boy that our dad had adopted before my brother and I had come there. My adoptive brother and my brother bonded and easily shared a room with one another.

Not long after my brother and I arrived had I begun to see my adoptive brother's true colors. A lot of the time our dad was at work, so after school we were all home alone. Sometimes my adoptive brother would close the door to the bathroom, turn off the lights, and scare the mess out of me with noises or his glow-in-the-dark Jason mask. To this day I don't understand how he got a kick out of that, but apparently he did. My adoptive brother's behavior began to worsen. Soon the scary stuff turned into sexual stuff. I was six so telling my father that my adoptive brother was doing these things to me was not only confusing, but it scared me. I didn't know what would happen or what my adoptive brother would do if I told and I didn't want to chance finding out.

A year later my dad asks me how I feel about having a sister. I was excited because I hadn't had a sister that was around the house before. My new sister was my adoptive brother's blood sister. When she first came she was nice and we played together but just like her brother; it didn't take long to see what kind of sister she planned on being. She began to bully me, if I didn't do the things that she wanted me to she would either threaten me or hurt me in some way. The things she wanted me to do usually resulted in me getting in trouble with my dad. I remember one time she wanted me to do something and I refused, then she punched me in my nose, making my nose bleed and then she told me to write "I want to die" with the blood from my nose on the bathroom mirror. After that incident my dad decided to have a family meeting without me and they all took a vote on whether I should leave or not. Everyone raised their hand including my brother.

My dad put me into a hospital and after about half a year I moved on to a group home in Virginia. Every time I talked to my dad or my brother I cried. They told me to be strong and not to cry… it never worked. I had been at the group home for almost a year when my social worker found a foster home for me in New Mexico. I went to this foster home and when it came time for me to leave I threw a fit. I was so tired of moving around. I hated it with a passion. It made me sick to think about it and I made it my job to try not to.

From that foster home I went into another. This lady social worker had moved into New Mexico around the time that I had and she started working at the agency that I was a foster child through. She became my Treatment Coordinator and she would visit my foster home and check my progress and just check on me. She was one of the people who had contributed to the decision that the last foster home wasn't good for me and that I needed to move.

On one of the visits that my social worker made every three months she had news to tell me. She told me that we were going to go to the park and then she would tell me the news. When we got to the park we sat down on a bench and she told me that I was going to be adopted. It was like a scene out of a movie because I screamed with happiness and birds flew away from the ground and the trees that were surrounding us. I hugged my social worker and then asked her who it was. I started guessing about what type of family was adopting and then she told me that it would be my Treatment Coordinator.

Living with my new mom was an experience for both of us. As I told you before, attaching to anyone was not ideal to me. Here was this woman who wanted to adopt me and wanted to become my mother and I was not even close to accepting her as a real friend. I would find little things to do that I believed would push my mother away. I stole, lied, played all kinds of games. Games like I couldn't sleep, making loud noises in the morning when I knew it got on her nerves, making little vocal noises and creating new twitches that would get me attention. I had put so much pain on her that others had caused me, had pushed my mother away so much, done so many things, that my ma was about to move on as well. She had called my social worker and told her that she had to let me go because I was too draining and difficult. My social worker then asked my ma if she'd be willing to go through a treatment program with me in another state. My ma said that she'd do what ever she could to help me.

In treatment I was considered one of the most stubborn kids that had gone through the program. I was so set in my ways that I was almost determined not to change or work on my life. The program was hard core and strict, so I eventually cracked. I was only supposed to be in the program for about three months; however my stubbornness had me there for six. While going through this program everything was pretty basic and strict. I said yes mom and yes dad to my temporary parents, did chores, ate and slept. When I wasn't doing those things I was sitting in a seat (kind of like a time-out). When I came home I was so scared that I was going to mess up and have to return back to the program. I was doing really well for about two months after I came home and then I started slipping up again. I was no longer following my heart and I began following my head. Trusting, loving, and putting my guard down for someone still terrified me. I went back to pushing my ma away because that was my passive way of showing her that I was scared. I was constantly getting in trouble because I figured that was the way to show my ma that I was not going to give in.

After a couple of years of struggling, therapy, stress, and tears I became tired of being unhappy. I was tired of making myself lonely and always being in trouble. I was ready to love my ma and I was ready to allow her to love me. I had seen that through all of the funk that I given her she was still there for me and with a love stronger than the pain that I had been feeling. I decided to give in and to be happy with the person that had taken me in when she really didn't have to.

I am now a senior in high school and I play volleyball for my varsity team. I will be the team captain this year and hopefully a scholarship will be a result of my volleyball skills. I'm seventeen years old now and I still have things to work on but I am working and my ma is still by my side working with me.

CHAPTER 8

When Children and Parents Need More

Sometimes, despite exhausting all known strategies and employing all known resources, you may find that you have hit a brick wall. Your child, and your family, is simply stuck—angry about the past, miserable in the present, and unable to move forward. At this point, the best intervention may be an out-of-home placement.

It may sound contradictory to suggest out-of-home placement as an intervention for disorders of attachment. How are you and your child to attach if you're not even living in the same place? It is a challenge, to be sure, but learning to develop a healthy relationship from a distance can be more productive than continuing the dance of an unhealthy relationship in close quarters. The key lies in how the out-of-home placement is managed.

Managed well, benefits of an out-of-home placement can include:

- Providing you and your child a "cooling off period."
- Enabling you to rest, rejuvenate, and build up your strength and motivation to continue the exhausting work of therapeutically parenting your child.
- Giving you the time and space to discover and learn new strategies for helping your child.

- Giving your child the opportunity to be more successful at expressing his feelings and choosing appropriate behaviors, due to being in a less-stressful environment (one in which nobody is trying to form a close relationship with him).

There are several options for out-of-home placements, including short-term respite care, long-term respite care, residential treatment centers (RTC) and psychiatric hospitalization. A qualified attachment therapist can guide you in determining which option is most appropriate for your situation.

Short-term respite care

Sometimes even a weekend apart can give both you and your child the renewed strength to keep going. Your local attachment therapist can steer you toward qualified, licensed respite providers, who are trained to work in their own homes with children who have extreme behaviors. These providers may not be in your immediate area, as some states do not have licensed respite providers and have limited access to these resources, but the distance is well worth traveling when you're at the end of your rope! You may need to seek respite resources through public child mental health or child welfare agencies, or through an adoptive parent group. Sometimes adoptive parents of older children, who have made progress in recovering from their attachment disorders, may be willing to provide informal respite support for other families.

It is important to position the decision to place your child in short-term respite care not as punishment, but as an opportunity for you to rest so that you can continue to have enough strength to help your child heal, and an opportunity for the child to have a break from you and to work on expressing his feelings and choosing appropriate behaviors with someone whose job it is to help children who need assistance in these areas.

Long-term respite care

For some families, the family dynamic is such that, even with qualified attachment therapy, the parents and child are simply unable to develop a healthy attachment, at least at that given point in time. In these cases, a therapist may recommend a longer-term placement in a respite home. The purpose of this is the same as for short-term respite care; however, it is typically the goal of long-term respite care for the child to develop an attachment to the respite care provider, which can then be transferred to his parents. Again, your attachment therapist can steer you toward qualified, licensed long-term respite care homes.

Psychiatric hospitalization

It is painful for any parent to consider placing a child in a psychiatric hospital; however, children who consistently behave in a manner that is dangerous to themselves or others are best served by being placed somewhere that has ample resources to keep them safe. Often this means psychiatric hospitalization. Psychiatric hospitalization enables a psychiatrist to observe the child's behavior over a period of time, rather than relying on weekly or monthly reports from the parent. Hospitalization also affords the psychiatrist the opportunity to monitor the child's medication daily, and to make changes in a safe environment. This may be necessary to arrive at an accurate diagnosis and, thus, an appropriate treatment plan. It is very important that the parent makes it clear to the child that the purpose of the hospitalization is safety. For example, "I cannot keep you safe right now and, as a good mom who loves you, I need to be sure that you (and we) are safe." Otherwise, the child may be "triggered" by the separation and perceive it as abandonment, rejection, or indication that the parent is not strong enough to handle the child's feelings.

Residential treatment centers

Some children exhibit such violent or dangerous behaviors that it is simply unmanageable for them to remain in a home, whether their own home or a respite home. In this case, a therapist may recommend the child be placed in a residential treatment center (RTC). RTCs are facilities that are staffed 24-hours per day, in shifts. RTCs are typically organized into cottages, each housing a small to medium group of same-gender children of similar ages, supervised by several staff members at all times. While living in an RTC, children typically attend school (either on or off campus), receive individual and group therapy, psychiatric evaluation and care, and participate in exercise and other group events. It is very important that the RTC's therapeutic program be focused on building attachments, or relationship skills, either between the child and a staff member, the child and the parent (this is possible if the parent lives close by and can spend significant time on campus) or even between the child and a peer (this is often an effective approach for teens). If the program focus is primarily behavioral, rather than on attachment or enhancing relationships, it is likely that the placement will not help a child who has a disorder of attachment and, in fact, it can often result in the child exhibiting even more extreme behaviors than he did prior to the placement. Again, placement in an RTC should never be positioned as punishment, but rather an intervention designed to help the child heal. It is important to explicitly state that the purpose of the placement is for safety and healing, and that the parent is not abandoning the child. The internal beliefs of children with disorders of attachment make them very vulnerable to perceiving separations as abandonment or "proof" that the caregiver does not love or want them.

Adoption disruptions and dissolutions

The vast majority of all adoptions—between 80 and 90%— are successful. However, sometimes a poor match is made or circumstances arise that make it impossible for an adoption to continue. When an adoption ends before it has been legally finalized in a courtroom, it is called a *disruption*. When a judge overturns an adoption after finalization it is called a *dissolution*, (although *disruption* is often used interchangeably to label both processes).

Which adoptions are at highest risk of failure?

In a nutshell, the older the child is at placement, the higher the risk of adoption disruption. It is extremely rare (less than 1 percent) for an infant adoption to disrupt, while 10 to 25 percent of domestic non-infant adoptions disrupt (U.S. Dept. of Health and Human Services 2004 report). While dissolution statistics are not readily available, it is estimated that less than 10 percent, and perhaps closer to 2 percent, of completed adoptions dissolve (The Child Welfare Information Gateway report, Evan B. Donaldson Adoption Institute report). However, age alone is not a reliable indicator. If a family is well prepared to adopt a 17-year-old teen, for instance, and the agency has offered full disclosure and supportive services, the adoption has an excellent chance to succeed in spite of the child's age. Adoption failure risk increases when proper adoption practices are not followed, and especially when the children being placed are older, troubled, and have been through one or more foster care placements, adoption disruptions or dissolutions before.

Why adoptions fail

When planning to adopt, parents typically imagine a life full of fun activities, travel, family gatherings, and living "happily ever after." Even when the parents are told in pre-adoption classes about significant potential issues related both to adoption in general and their prospective child specifically, it is nearly impossible for them to imagine what the reality may truly be. To help prospective adoptive parents develop more realistic expectations, they should read as much as they can about adoption issues and attend classes in attachment and bonding. In addition, the family needs to form a support network, including forming connections with local parent support groups, and identifying a variety of resources that may be necessary, such as an attachment therapist, psychiatrist, social skills classes, and respite care. The time for preparation is *before* the child is placed in the home.

Once the child joins the family, a wide variety of unexpected issues may emerge, such as significant developmental delays or extreme behaviors. Conflict may build between spouses over how best to respond to these challenges. In many cases, a child who has a disorder of attachment may act very differently toward the primary caregiver than toward the other parent, so that the parents' perspectives on what is happening are vastly different. Conflict between the newly arrived child and children already in the home may increase beyond expected or appropriate levels. The child who has a disorder of attachment may feel very jealous of other children who can more easily connect with the parent or who did not have to go through the same traumatic experiences as he did. He may also feel threatened by the other children's needs, believing that his own needs may not be met. He may never verbalize these feelings, and may even deny them, but these feelings may add significant stress to the family system. In some cases, the situation may be dangerous, even life threatening, for the child or a sibling. Parents need to be able to recognize early when the family needs help creating and maintaining a healthy home environment, and engage the appropriate resources immediately. They also need to have the financial resources in place in advance to fund these resources.

Adoption failure is less likely to occur when:

- The adoption agency is licensed, recommended by adoption support groups, and maintains high standards of service and ethics.
- Families are well-prepared to adopt and raise the child(ren) being placed.
- The match between child and parents is sound, respecting the needs, personalities, and strengths of all parties.
- Full disclosure is given to parents about the child's history, diagnosis, and special needs.
- Post-adoption services and, when available, financial assistance, are in place to support the family.
- Crisis intervention services are available if needed.
- The parents have ongoing access to the help of the social worker who made the match and placed the child.

When it comes to adoption, there are no guarantees of success, of course, because every situation is unique. However, when these factors are present, the likelihood of adoption success is very high.

Considering disruption/dissolution

When is disruption really necessary? Adopting children is not like buying shoes. You can't try a pair on for size, discard it if the fit or appearance isn't perfect, and go on to the next pair. But sometimes disruption/dissolution is unavoidable. If you are considering disruption/dissolution, ask yourself two questions, and proceed with disruption/dissolution if the answer to both is "yes:"

1. Is any member of your family in danger of ongoing serious physical or psychological trauma? (This applies to human members only, not pets.)
2. Have you tried everything possible to keep the family intact (e.g., medication, a different therapeutic approach, safety devices such as window/room alarms, residential treatment, psychiatric hospitalization)?

It is important to keep in mind that there are many ways to safely parent a child who has dangerous behaviors, if a family is willing to work to find solutions. However, this is not as easy as it sounds. It is often difficult to find the patience and energy to go on, after confronting the realization that your preparation was insufficient to meet the needs of the child, and being exhausted by feelings of bewilderment, numbness, confusion, loss of sleep, and the daily frustration of attempting to manage—often unsuccessfully—the child's behaviors. You may also feel overwhelmed by the totally unexpected amount of financial resources required to fund all of the child's needs. Because you may vacillate between feeling depressed one day and confident the next, keeping a journal of behaviors and interventions, and the success thereof, is an invaluable tool. A journal can help you and the professionals from whom you seek help to more accurately identify patterns and issues, and thus determine the next most appropriate step.

The emotions of a failing adoption

If you are considering disruption/dissolution, you are most certainly overwhelmed by a plethora of powerful emotions, all of which make it extremely difficult to think clearly and function well.

Anger

You may experience anger toward God, the adoption agency/orphanage, social workers, the birth family, caregivers, or other people involved in "damaging" your child. You may feel angry toward your child for making you and your family members miserable, or angry at your spouse, close friends or family members for lack of support or for lack of acceptance and understanding.

Guilt

You may feel guilty or ashamed about not being able to parent the child effectively, about having ambivalent feelings toward your child, and about choosing to bring your child's negative influence into the family. You may be too embarrassed or too caught up in the situation to reach out for help from other experienced parents or from a therapist. You may be plagued by self-doubt and a loss of confidence in parenting skills.

Loneliness

You may feel as though no one else has any idea of how you feel or what you are experiencing. Due to your child's behaviors, you may not participate in activities as often as you did before. You may fear there is something wrong with you, and may hesitate to share these feelings of inadequacy with a therapist, fearing that you will be considered a poor parent.

Clinical Depression

Clinical depression is not uncommon when an adoption is at risk of failure. Following are some common symptoms of depression:

- Unremitting feelings of frustration, isolation, hopelessness, lack of motivation, and/or helplessness.
- A noticeable inability to maintain a positive mood.
- Conversations with friends seem shallow and unimportant.

- Abandonment of previously established stress relievers, such as exercise, social interaction with other adults, or recreational activities.
- Headaches, nervousness, forgetfulness
- Lack of sleep, lack of energy
- Lack of appetite or uncontrollable eating
- Digestive problems and/or ulcers
- Suicidal thoughts

These emotions cannot be managed alone. It is critical to have professional guidance to help sort through these issues and emotions to find the truly best course of action for your child and your family.

The legal side of disruption/dissolution

If the adoption has not yet been finalized, the process of disruption is quite simple. You may sign papers declaring that the adoption has been reversed and that you are no longer responsible for your child's welfare. Any adoption subsidy payments to you stop as of the day your child leaves home. No court involvement is necessary to disrupt during the adoption process.

If the adoption has already been finalized, you must have your parental rights legally terminated, which requires court involvement. In the case of teens and severely emotionally disturbed children, a judge will sometimes refuse to grant dissolution and opt for an alternative that allows the family to remain intact but live apart. In many states, the judge can order the state to take physical custody of the child until age 18 for purposes of obtaining outpatient treatment that is unavailable to the family privately. The family can visit and remain involved with treatment decisions. Sometimes, you are required to make child support payments until your child is adopted by someone else or turns 18 years old. There are cases where child support is required past the age of 18 and/or until high school graduation. Federal law allows parents to retain adoption assistance as long as they have parental rights, and contribute in some way to the child's support. This assistance can be used to make child support payments.

Passage of a federal law in the year 2000 that made citizenship faster and easier for internationally adopted children also created new ramifications surrounding disruption. People who adopt children from other countries and bring them back into the USA must sign a form pledging to be financially responsible for the child. Form I-864, the Affidavit of Support, requires that adoptive parents reimburse any government or private agency that provides their child with any means-tested public benefit, such as food stamps or welfare.

Under no circumstances should you proceed with a disruption or dissolution without agency or a private lawyer involvement, to guide you through the legal issues and steps. Following are a few examples of ways in which parents may make poor, and in some cases legally actionable, decisions without the help of legal counsel:

- Returning the child to the country of birth, if internationally adopted, is not a moral option, unless the agency has made arrangements for the child to be adopted there by a qualified family or relative.
- The return of any child to their country of birth must also include the involvement of the Department of State, Office of Children's Issue and Central Authority. International treaties and laws must be adhered to regarding the transfer of children between countries.
- Moving the child to the home of another family without agency help is very risky. The new family has no legal rights and will have difficulty obtaining medical care or enrolling the child in school without official adoption papers.
- Moving a child across state lines without the involvement of the ICPC (Interstate Compact on the Placement of Children) officers of both states is illegal. The ICPC is charged with monitoring the movement of all children across state lines when their legal parents will not accompany them permanently.
- Some parents may be advised by well-meaning friends not to pick up a troubled child from a shelter, psychiatric hospital, or residential treatment. Refusing to do so will most likely result in the parents incurring charges of abandonment of a child. Even when it is unsafe for other family members to bring a troubled child home, the District Attorney will not approve of disruption by abandonment. Parents are expected to go through proper legal channels.

Helping your child through a disruption/dissolution

It is so important to put your child's best interests first throughout the process of disruption or dissolution. "Best interests" has been legally defined as "safety first," which includes psychological safety. You must gently inform your child that he will not be able to continue living at home, but that he will have a safe place to live, with enough food, and people to care for him. A therapist can help you find the right words that are honest, age-appropriate, and framed as kindly as possible. For example, it is much better to tell a child that continuing the adoption is not safe for everyone, than to tell him that the adoption is over because he starts fires. There will be time later, in therapy, to address the behaviors that caused the disruption. At this stage, the child needs to know that he will continue to be cared for and that the decision is difficult but necessary.

The weeks spanning the decision, the actual changeover to a new home, and the initial weeks following are emotionally charged with many feelings. These include grief at the loss of the dream "forever" family, anxiety over the child's response to the decision, guilt while listening to the child make future plans, and knowing that the future is about to be torn away from the child. The changeover preparation process can be overwhelmingly emotional— gathering information for the new family, dealing with fond memories attached to photos, communicating the decisions to others, deciding what to say to whom and when, and then setting up the scenario for announcement, leave-taking, and actual departure. In some cases, the child may express pleasure and excitement about going to a new family and getting away from the uncomfortable first family. In other cases, the child may go into rages over a sense of betrayal and loss of control. Parents must manage their own emotional travail while helping the child and siblings to adjust to the sudden change in life plans.

A therapist who specializes in adoption, or an adoption professional with disruption experience, can help the parents make a transition plan that best meets the needs of all the family members, including the children remaining in the home. Agencies and professionals should plan for all possible scenarios and implement strategies to address as many as possible.

When it actually comes time for the child to leave, parents should pack the child's belongings in suitcases and backpacks, not garbage bags and sacks. Garbage should go into garbage bags, not a child's possessions. Care should be taken to remember all of the child's belongings, including the adoption lifebook or scrapbook. You are part of the child's past forever, and he will want to have mementos of his time with you, including photographs. Give these personal items to the child's social worker who will decide when it is appropriate to give them to the child. Make sure the child eats a good meal before the social worker arrives to take him to his next placement. Make the good-byes short, simple, and as calm as possible. The final words should be honest, positive, and recognize the feelings that are present. For example, you might say something like, "Susan, I am sorry that the adoption cannot continue. I know you are sad. We are sad, too, but we believe that this is the best thing to do. I hope that you are very happy in your next home. You have a beautiful smile so let your new family see that smile everyday. Good-bye, Susan."

After leaving your home, the child is placed in a foster home, treatment center, or shelter while long-term plans are made by the agency. If the next adoptive family has been identified, the child may go there directly. In most cases, efforts will be made to return the child to the last foster home where things are familiar. The good news is that most children who have experienced a disruption will go on to have a successful adoption with another family.

After the disruption/dissolution

Give yourself time to grieve. The emotional pain of a disruption has been compared to that of a miscarriage or stillbirth. Obviously, no one dies as the result of a failed adoption, but something dies—the parent-child relationship. The dream of raising this son or daughter evaporates. In one moment, the future is changed forever. You were a parent and now you are not. Intense grief for the loss of a child/sibling is accompanied by feelings of intense relief from the constant acting out, readjusting to the revised family unit, nurturing yourself and other family members, while thinking of the new hope for the child in a different family. You struggle with the question of "why" the situation happened. Thoughts of "if I had only" plague you, as you work through accepting your inability to successfully parent this child.

You and your other children, if any, must cope with sharing your painful news and coping with others' questions. Grief can arise at unexpected times. Families can benefit from working with a therapist or adoption professional with disruption experience to help recognize and process the loss, relief, and related feelings. If the child was violent or acted out seriously against one or more family members, you and your other children may have post-traumatic stress issues, and may need to address them with a professional. Keep the lines of communication open, especially with your other children. Reassure them over and over that the disruption is not their fault. They may need to hear this many times. Explain to them in simple and honest ways why the disruption was necessary. If they are adopted, they may wonder if their adoptions might be disrupted next, and need assurance that this is not the case. Children can make strange assumptions (e.g., worry that they too might do something that would cause them to have to leave), so it is important to listen to their feelings and answer their questions. Grandparents and other extended family members must also grieve the loss after a disruption. Knowing it was best for all concerned does not change the fact that a loss has occurred. There are feelings of sadness, disbelief, anger, relief, and guilt. It takes time to work through these feelings.

Some experts say it takes six to twelve months for families to resolve the loss, while others suggest it may take at least half the amount of time the child was with the family. The family counselor, individual counselor, other parents with disruption experience, school counselors and children's adult mentors can all help with recovery of the original family unit, and the adjustment to new realities. As with any grief/loss scenario, the hurt eases over time, with certain activities or holidays triggering new waves of loss. The grief is somewhat cyclical, getting better week by week, and then seeming to overwhelm the new reality. Counselors can help parents understand how children process grief differently from adults and how to encourage children who remain in the family unit to express their grief, anger, or abandonment concerns through storytelling, drawing, and writing.

As you work toward self-forgiveness, processing the events and decisions that led to the disruption/dissolution, you begin to accept that you are stronger because parenting skills, relationships, and inner resources have been thoroughly tested. Some children, thinking that they will be next to leave, may begin acting out. Your remaining children need to process conflicting feelings of loss and relief, as well as be reassured by you of their permanency in the family. Children need time (sometimes years) to let go of anger toward you—especially if you are the mother, as primary attachment figure—and to forgive you for sending their sibling away and making them feel vulnerable.

Disruption is the death of an adoption and the end of a dream, but it is not necessarily the end of love. Adoptive parents often anguish over the future welfare of the children who were once theirs. With most agencies, it is standard policy to give the parents no information at all on the children after disruption. Some families are advised to have no initial contact while the child adjusts to the new family, perhaps as long as six months to a year. This encourages the child to focus on the new family rather than a fantasy of returning to the first family, and allows the first family to readjust to their new reality.

Other families find contact between the new and old families to be beneficial for both. The first parents can be reassured that the child is adjusting, and the new parents have a resource for insights into the care of the child. The child may need reassurance from the first family that they still care about him. Siblings may be reassured by hearing from one another, or it may cause renewed feelings of loss and resentment toward the first parents. The new parents will need to be in control of this communication, in consultation with their therapists and post-placement supervisor.

In some states, privacy laws leave the agency no choice. However, when it is possible to share information, it can help both the parents and the child through the grieving process, easing their minds and helping them move toward closure.

Adopting another child after a disruption/dissolution

As with other loss/grief scenarios, it may be advisable for the family to wait at least a year before considering another adoption. This gives the family dynamic several seasons of activity to regain a sense of normalcy, rebuilding relationships and strengthening bonds that were strained by the situation with the child who is now in another family.

At some point, the family may indeed choose to pursue another adoption, and should be prepared to address issues related to the failure of the first placement, not only from the adoption professionals involved, but also for the family and friends who have watched previous struggles, and will be concerned on behalf of the family.

Many parents assume that adoption disruption/dissolution in their families will prevent them from ever adopting again. This is not true! Adoption agencies approve adoption applications based on the outcome of the adoption home study or assessment. If the assessment shows that the dissolution was necessary, that the parents acted responsibly, and that they are capable of providing a good home for another child, the application will likely be approved. Obviously, a family that has experienced more than one disruption/dissolution will be more carefully scrutinized, but even then, it is important to remember that each case is considered individually. You cannot know whether you will be approved until you try.

In many cases, surviving a disruption/dissolution makes a family an even better candidate for a successful adoption on the next attempt. Why? Because this family has been through a painful process of self-examination. They know what they can handle and what they can't. They have experience and are better able to determine if they are the right match for a particular child.

Disruption/dissolution stories

When facing disruption with our two children we felt we had made a decision to dissolve the relationship with them. After contacting a lawyer we discovered the financial strain was more than we felt our already fragile couple relationship could take. We are thankful to a judge who was willing to confront the state and demand they solve the problem without dissolving our parental rights. With the judge's pressure we were able to find state support which allowed our children to stay in our parental custody while being in state custody. I feel our children benefited from knowing we were still their parents even though they did not live with us again.

It has been my privilege to successfully adopt nine children, but along the way, I have also experienced two disruptions: one after three days, and one after four months. These were older children who had experienced other disruptions and were at high risk due to dangerous behaviors, so there was a strong statistical probability of failure. Unfortunately, being statistically predictable did nothing to alleviate the intense emotional pain of these two losses. Even though they occurred almost 20 years ago, I still think of them with sadness. But then I remember the nine adoptions that have worked, and my three grandchildren, and I realize that this is part of the risk we have to take to open our hearts and homes to certain children. Is older child or special needs adoption worth it, even with the risk of disruption? Each individual parent must find the answer to this question for himself or herself. For me, the answer is yes, times nine.

This section on disruptions and dissolutions is based on the articles *From Adoption to Solution or Dissolution: Supporting Families During Emotional Stages of Challenging Adoptions*, by Rebecca Dinkins and Bernadine Janzen (2/25/06), and *A Parent's Guide to Adoption Disruptions and Dissolutions*.

APPENDIX A

Choosing an Attachment Therapist

This appendix contains a series of questions that you can use to help evaluate whether a therapist is qualified to treat children with disorders of attachment and in general a good fit for your family.

Professional qualifications

Does the therapist:

- Have a current license/certification or other credential required by their particular state?
- Belong to ATTACh (Association for Treatment and Training in the Attachment of Children)?
- Have a current clinical registered membership in ATTACh (see attach.org) or meet the standards to be a registered clinician (80 hours of specialized post-graduate training in the diagnosis and treatment of disorders of attachment and regular continuing education in those areas)?

- Have a current membership in his/her professional organization, and follow the organization's established code of ethics and standards of practice?

Training questions

- What training has the therapist received specific to attachment, trauma, early childhood development, adoption, foster care, and family therapy?
- How long has the therapist been practicing? How long has the therapist been treating children with disorders of attachment? Is 50% of the therapist's practice with adopted and foster children and others with disorders of attachment?
- Is the therapist skilled in treating a variety of problems with a variety of techniques? For example, comfortable in facilitating attachment building, working on behavior management strategies, working with ADHD and/or learning disabilities, helping with grief work, PTSD, Bipolar disorder, treating sexual abuse issues and helping with adoption related issues?
- How many hours of supervised and "hands on training" under the mentorship of a qualified attachment therapist does the therapist have?
- Does the therapist continue to learn about new developments in attachment therapy through a minimum of 10 continuing education units annually and maintain contact with other professionals in the field?
- Does the therapist have peer and professional consultation a minimum of 1 hour per month?

Therapeutic process questions

- What ages does the therapist serve?
- Under what circumstances would the therapist choose not to treat a child/family?
- What are the treatment philosophies/goals of the therapist?
- How long is the usual course of therapy?

- Does the initial assessment of the child/family follow accepted guidelines of ATTACh?
- How many therapists are part of the therapeutic process?
- What attention is given to educating parents with regard to specialized attachment parenting?
- What attention is given to helping parents heal their own emotional issues?
- Does the therapist make and use a contract between the therapist(s) and the parent(s), between the parent(s) and the child, and between the child and the therapist(s)?
- Is treatment done with the parent(s) present and joining with the therapist(s) on behalf of the child? Are parents considered a part of the treatment team?
- Does the clinician work with the family and community to find supports for respite?
- How does the therapist maintain coordination and continuity of care among various providers?
- Is the clinician willing to participate in community meetings that involve the child's welfare (e.g., school, court/probation, child welfare)?
- Does the therapist's orientation include what has become known as an "Intensive" (a duration of consecutive days of therapeutic treatment)?
- If "Intensives" are used what is the therapeutic rationale for it (the "Intensive")? What follow-up work is provided after an "Intensive"?
- If a child is from out of town, is there an arrangement made for a follow-up therapist in the child's local area? Is the hometown therapist invited to participate in the therapeutic process?
- Is the therapist willing to refer for additional assessments (for example, speech and hearing, sensory integration, medical and neurological evaluations)?
- If holding techniques are utilized, who does the holding and what style is used? Is nurturing holding an important part of the treatment? ATTACh does not support intrusive, provocative, and coercive methods of treatment—see ATTACh's Position Paper (posted at attach.org, About ATTACh, Position Papers).
- What is the therapist's specific plan to keep everyone safe (see Attach's Safety Principles (posted at attach.org)?

Financial considerations

- How much does treatment cost?
- What funding sources are available to assist in the cost of treatment?
- Does the therapist accept insurance? If so, with which programs does the therapist participate?

APPENDIX B

Fact Sheet for Educators

Children with disorders of attachment are often the victims of abuse, neglect, abandonment, physical illness, multiple placements and/or in-utero drug/alcohol exposure. Their problems are rooted in the first five years of their lives, when trauma occurred. Stable attachments cannot be formed when a child experiences frequent changes in day care or foster care, or when the child's social, emotional, physical, and cognitive needs are unmet.

While many children with disorders of attachment have grown up in foster care and/or adoptive homes, these disorders occur in children who are growing up with their biological families as well. An inordinate number of school children in the United States have disorders of attachment due to divorce, separation from parents (e.g., military service), inappropriate day care programs, and multiple caregivers. Children who have experienced medical events such as hospitalization, placement in an incubator, or a body cast can also develop these disorders.

Children who have lived in violent or chaotic homes often have not experienced seeing their behaviors result in logical consequences. They may not have acquired the tools needed to succeed in school because they had to focus all of their efforts on surviving their traumatic experiences. The consistency required for children to learn effectively is frequently absent in the homes of neglected and abused children. In addition, in order to cope with traumatic experiences, some children dissociate (separate their consciousness from their bodies). Even when the child is in a safe environment, stress (such as having to speak in front of a class) will often trigger a dissociative episode. Children who dissociate in class miss a lot of information, even though they are physically present.

Children who have been traumatized use both spacing out (dissociating) and acting out to survive their classroom experiences. They spend less time being focused on their lessons. Children with disorders of attachment sometimes do not respect authority, especially that of their parents. They can be oppositional and defiant in the school setting, although many behave perfectly with those who are not parenting them. It is not uncommon for a child with a disorder of attachment to be a good student as well as the most helpful child in the class. The same child may go home and exhibit acting out, or even violent, behavior.

Children with disorders of attachment lack the ability to trust. Their behavior meets their subconscious need to keep those who love them most at a distance. They are fearful that, if they become emotionally close to their parents, they will somehow be hurt again as they were in the past. They are terrified of closeness, and will do anything they can to create distance between themselves and their parents.

One way this is manifested is in children's ability to triangulate, that is, to pit one adult against the other. Children with disorders of attachment sometimes lie to their teachers, accusing their parents of emotional abuse, physical abuse or neglect, and lie so convincingly that their teachers believe them. Many parents have been erroneously reported for suspected child abuse when school personnel have listened to the child without checking the facts with the parent. Without violating mandatory reporting requirements, teachers can subtly investigate a child's allegation without accusing the parent. For example, if a child reports that he does not have a lunch because his parent refused to give him one, a teacher could call the parent and ask, "Did Johnny forget his lunch today?" Children may also lie to their parents about their teachers. It is critically important for parents and teachers of children with disorders of attachment to keep in constant contact with one another, to avoid misunderstandings and false allegations.

What's a teacher to do?

1. Develop and maintain constant communication with the child's parents. This will greatly increase the chance of all adults being consistent in the child's life at home and at school. Be sure to check with parents if you suspect that the child's story could be untrue. Ask parents to do the same for you. For example, if the child comes home and says that his teacher hit him, yelled at him or otherwise behaved inappropriately, please ask the parents to check out the child's story with you before acting upon it.
2. In order to feel safe, children with disorders of attachment need a tightly structured, loving environment. They do not need an overly permissive environment which makes them feel unsafe.
3. Teachers must respect the need of the parents to be the primary attachment figures in this child's life. When parents and teachers do not communicate with one another effectively, children with disorders of attachment will feel frightened and insecure. The child who is able to triangulate, by keeping parents and teachers at odds with one another, will feel insecure in the home and school environments.
4. It is critically important to follow through on any and all consequences. The child's safety and that of others depends on it.
5. Hold the child responsible for his actions. Understand that, until the child's behavior becomes more positive, he will have an extremely depressing life. Even though the child has problems and may have a painful past, it is important to hold him responsible for his actions and to provide logical, reasonable consequences.
6. Teachers must understand that, if the child asks to go home with them after criticizing his parents, this is a means of distancing from closeness with the parents. The child may be fearful of closeness with parents because previous parents have abandoned or traumatized him, not because his current parents are abusive or neglectful.

7. Children with disorders of attachment sometimes need to regress and experience the close care and nurturing they missed as young children, especially during times of stress. As their emotional needs are met, their social-emotional development will become more age-appropriate. Teachers must realize that there are days when a child may need to stay home from school because he simply needs to be close to his parents that day. Once disorders of attachment are resolved, the child will have plenty of energy to make up for lost time at school.

Classroom strategies

1. Remain proactive. Set the tone for the work expected of the child.
2. Adults need to give neutral emotional responses. If a teacher acts angry, shocked, or punitive in the classroom, the child will feel unsafe.
3. Avoid control battles; give firm, clear expectations.
4. Acknowledge choices and consequences. If the child chooses not to cooperate, the adult states the possible consequences of that choice.
5. Convey commitment and perseverance. Children with disorders of attachment have often learned to "wait the other person out," realizing that they can succeed in controlling adults who have become frustrated, confused, or hopeless in dealing with them. Give them the message that adults will persevere, no matter how long it takes.
6. Do not resist the resistance. Project an air of indifference regarding the behavior (not the child).
7. Identify the child's underlying emotions. Children with disorders of attachment are generally resistant because they are anxious and/or fearful. When teachers display genuine concern and compassion for these underlying emotions, the focus changes from superficial manipulation to meaningful expressions of emotion.
8. Typically, children's cooperation increases when they know they will be rewarded. Samples of rewards include one tiny piece of candy placed covertly on a child's desk, or a one-minute break that includes walking around. However, behavior

modification techniques are often unsuccessful with children with disorders of attachment.

9. Teachers can encourage, validate, empower, and guide children to success and rapport. They must convey the message, "I know you can do this; you can be a winner."
10. If a child is so disruptive that he must be removed from the classroom, he should be escorted by an adult to a quiet location where he can work on an assignment. Children with disorders of attachment should never be sent away from the classroom alone, or made to stand outside alone, which re-ignites fears of abandonment and may create feelings of shame.

Goals for children with disorders of attachment, at school and in the home

1. Children will learn to acknowledge and express a range of difficult emotions (anger, fear, sadness, pain, guilt, and shame) in a direct and genuine manner.
2. They will learn to take responsibility for their actions and decisions. They will learn to solve problems and make pro-social choices.
3. It is important for children with disorders of attachment to develop positive regard (trust, respect, and caring) toward themselves. They will thereby reduce the self-contempt which is associated with their negative, internal beliefs.
4. The tone of the classroom must encourage respectful behavior. Teachers model this by being respectful of their students and other adults in the classroom. Children can be encouraged to show respect by maintaining good eye contact, by doing things quickly when asked, and by not interrupting.
5. Children can demonstrate responsibility by taking care of their bodies, belongings, and assignments. This means that they will be encouraged to keep their hands to themselves, keep their desks clean, handle school responsibilities, finish work before play, and take care of their feelings in an age-appropriate matter.
6. Children with disorders of attachment can learn to be polite, do assignments promptly and correctly, remain quiet, listen when others talk, avoid arguments,

play calmly, offer help to others, and be honest. All of these goals can be accomplished in a small, academically challenging classroom with a low adult to child ratio. Effective communication between school personnel and parents is vitally important.

Tool for managing extreme behaviors

Following is a sample tool that can be used to manage and process extreme behaviors in the classroom:

FFP Respite/School Tool

Youth's name:____________________________ Date:____________________

PROBLEM BEHAVIORS: These are behaviors I sometimes show, especially when I'm stressed:

- ☐ Losing control
- ☐ Assaulting people
- ☐ Leaving to be alone
- ☐ Running away
- ☐ Using other drugs
- ☐ Injuring myself
- ☐ Attempting suicide
- ☐ Threatening others
- ☐ Using alcohol
- ☐ Feeling unsafe
- ☐ Other (please describe): ____________________

TRIGGERS: When these things happen, I am more likely to feel unsafe and upset:

- ☐ Not being listened to
- ☐ Feeling pressured
- ☐ Being touched
- ☐ Lack of privacy
- ☐ People yelling
- ☐ Loud noises
- ☐ Feeling lonely
- ☐ Arguments
- ☐ Not having control
- ☐ Being isolated
- ☐ Darkness
- ☐ Being stared at
- ☐ Being teased
- ☐ Particular time of day: ____________
- ☐ Particular time of year: ____________
- ☐ Contact with family
- ☐ Particular person: ____________
- ☐ Other (please describe): ____________________

WARNING SIGNS: These are things other people may notice me doing if I begin to lose control:

- ☐ Sweating
- ☐ Breathing hard
- ☐ Racing heart
- ☐ Clenching teeth
- ☐ Clenching fists
- ☐ Red faced
- ☐ Wringing hands
- ☐ Loud voice
- ☐ Sleeping a lot
- ☐ Sleeping less
- ☐ Acting hyper
- ☐ Swearing
- ☐ Bouncing legs
- ☐ Rocking
- ☐ Can't sit still
- ☐ Being rude
- ☐ Pacing
- ☐ Crying
- ☐ Squatting
- ☐ Hurting things
- ☐ Eating more
- ☐ Eating less
- ☐ Not taking care of myself
- ☐ Isolating/avoiding people
- ☐ Laughing loudly/giddy
- ☐ Singing inappropriately
- ☐ Other (please describe): ____________________

INTERVENTIONS: These are things that might help me calm down and keep myself safe when I'm feeling upset:
(Check off what you know works; star things you might like to try in the future)

- ☐ Time out in my room
- ☐ Listening to music
- ☐ Reading a book
- ☐ Sitting with staff
- ☐ Pacing
- ☐ Talking with Friends
- ☐ Talking with an adult
- ☐ Coloring
- ☐ Molding clay
- ☐ Humor
- ☐ Exercising
- ☐ A cold cloth on face
- ☐ Writing in a journal
- ☐ Hugging a stuffed animal
- ☐ Drinking hot herb tea
- ☐ Taking a hot shower
- ☐ Taking a cold shower
- ☐ Playing cards
- ☐ Video Games
- ☐ Lying down
- ☐ Calling family (who?)
- ☐ Holding ice in my hand
- ☐ Getting a hug
- ☐ Using the gym
- ☐ Using a rocking chair
- ☐ Bouncing a ball
- ☐ Male staff support
- ☐ Female staff support
- ☐ Deep breathing
- ☐ Speaking w/my therapist
- ☐ Drawing
- ☐ Being read a story
- ☐ Making a collage
- ☐ Crying
- ☐ Snapping bubble wrap
- ☐ Being around others
- ☐ Doing chores/jobs
- ☐ Cold water on hands
- ☐ Other (please describe): ____________________

Foster Family Programs of Hawaii

THINGS THAT MAKE IT WORSE: These are things that do NOT help me calm down or stay safe:

- ☐ Being alone
- ☐ Being around people
- ☐ Sarcasm
- ☐ Not being listened to
- ☐ Peers teasing
- ☐ Being disrespected
- ☐ Loud tone of voice
- ☐ Being ignored
- ☐ Having staff support
- ☐ Talking to an adult
- ☐ Being reminded of the rules
- ☐ Being touched
- ☐ Other (please describe): ______________________

CRISIS PLAN:

1) I will try to notice the following warning signs and triggers:

2) I'd like staff/my family to notice the following warning signs:

3) When I notice these triggers or warning signs, I will take action to prevent a crisis from developing by doing the following:

4) When staff/my family notice that I'm getting upset, I'd like them to help me prevent a crisis by doing the following:

Youth signature ______________________ Date: __________

Parent signature ______________________ Date: __________

Parent signature ______________________ Date: __________

Worker signature ______________________ Date: __________

Foster Family Programs of Hawaii

This form can be downloaded from the ATTACh website (attach.org).

Alternative classroom placements

In some cases, children with disorders of attachment simply cannot function in a standard public school classroom, due to the severity of their behaviors. In these cases, placement in a special class or therapeutic day school can be helpful. In the most extreme cases, placement in a residential treatment facility may be required. See "Psychiatric hospitalization" on page 95 for more information.

APPENDIX C Resources

Bibliography

Amen, Daniel G., M.D., *Change Your Brain Change Your Life*, Three Rivers Press, New York, 1998, ISBN# 0-8129-2998-5.

Amen, Daniel G., M.D., *Images of Human Behavior*, ISBN# 1-88655404-8.

Anisworth, Mary, *Patterns of Attachment*, Lawrence Erlbaum Associates, 1978.

Bailey, Becky A., Ph.D., *I Love You Rituals.*

Becker-Weidman, Arthur, Ph.D. and Shell, Deborah, MA, Editors, *Creating Capacity for Attachmen*t.

Bowlby, John, *Attachment and Loss, Volumes I-III*, Basic Books, New York, 1980.

Bowlby, John, *A Secure Base*, Basic Books, 1998.

Brazelton, T. Berry, M.D. and Greenspan, Stanley I., M.D., *The Irreducible Needs of Children*.

Brodzinsky, David M., Ph.D., Schechter, Marshall D., M.D., and Henig, Robin Marantz, *Being Adopted, The Lifelong Search for Self.*

Cournos, Francine, *City of One*, W.W. Norton & Company Inc., New York, NY, ISBN# 0-393-04731-8.

Delaney, Richard J., Ph.D., *Safe Passages*.

Eldridge, Sherrie, *Twenty Things Adopted Kids Wish Their Adoptive Parents Knew*, Dell Publishing, 1999, ISBN# 0-440-50838-X.

Eshleman, Lark, Ph.D., *Becoming a Family: Promoting Healthy Attachments with Your Adopted Child*, Taylor Publishing Company, 2004.

Faber, Adele and Mazlish, Elaine, *How to Talk So Kids & Listen So Kids Will Talk*, Library of Congress 2004, ISBN# 0-380-81196-0.

Faber, Adele and Mazlish, Elaine, *How to Talk So Teens Will Listen & Listen So Teens Will Talk*, Library of Congress, ISBN-10# 0-06-074125-2, ISBN-13# 0-06-074125-2.

Faber, Adele and Mazlish, Elaine, *Siblings Without Rivalry,* Library of Congress 2004, ISBN# 0-380-79900-6.

Fisher, Antwone, *Finding Fish*, Harper Torch, New York, NY, 2001, ISBN# 0-06-053986-0.

Forbes, Heather T., LCSW and Post, B. Bryan, Ph.D., LCSW, *Beyond Consequences, Logic and Control.*

Gray, Deborah D., *Attaching in Adoption: Practical Tools for Today's Parents*, Perspectives Press, Indianapolis, IN, 2002, ISBN# 0-944934-29-3.

Gray, Steven, Ph.D., *The Maltreated Child*, Living Water Press, Colorado Springs, CO, 2004, ISBN# 9746412-0-0-0.

Green, Ross, Ph.D., *The Explosive Child: A New Approach for Understanding and Parenting Easily Frustrated, Chronically Inflexible Children*, 2005.

Hughes, Daniel A., *Facilitating Developmental Attachment*, Jason Aronson, Inc., NY, NJ, 1997, ISBN# 0-7657-0038-7.

Hughes, Daniel A., *Building the Bonds of Attachment: Awakening Love in Deeply Troubled Children, 2nd Edition*, 2006.

Jernberg, Ann M. and Booth, Phyllis B., *Theraplay: Helping Parents and Children Build Better Relationships Through Attachment-Based Play*, Library of Congress, ISBN# 0-7879-4302-9.

Karen, Robert, Ph.D., *Becoming Attached.*

Keck, Gregory C., Ph.D. and Kupecky, Regina M.,LSW, *Parenting the Hurt Child.*

Keck, Gregory C., Ph.D. and Kupecky, Regina M., LSW, *Adopting the Hurt Child.*

Klaus, Marshall and Kennell, John, *Bonding, The Beginning of Parent-Infant Attachment*, ISBN# 0-8016-2696-4.

Klaus, Marshall; Kennell, John; and Klaus, Phyllis, *Bonding: Building the Foundations of a Secure Attachment and Independence*,1995.

Kranowitz Stock, Carol, M.A., *The Out-of Sync Child: Recognizing and Coping with Sensory Integration Dysfunction*, Berkley Publishing Group, New York, 1998.

Lacher, Denise; Nichols, Todd; and May, Joanne C., *Connecting with Kids through Stories*, Jessica Kingsley Publishers, London UK., ISBN# 1-84310-797-X.

Levy, Terry and Orlans, Michael, *Attachment, Trauma, and Healing*, CWLA Press, Washington, D.C., 1998, ISBN# 0-87868-709-2.

Orlans, Michael, M.A. and Levy, Terry, Ph.D., *Healing Parents: Helping Wounded Children Learn to Trust & Love*.

Perry, Bruce D., M.D., Ph.D. and Szalavitz, Maia, *The Boy Who Was Raised As a Dog: And Other Stories from a Child Psychiatrist's Notebook—What Traumatized Children Can Teach Us About Loss, Love, and Healing*.

Siegel, Daniel, M.D. and Hartzell, Mary, *Parenting from the Inside Out*, Jeremy P. Tarcher/Penguin, New York, N.Y., 2003, ISBN#1-58542-295-9.

Trout, Michael and Thomas, Lori, *The Jonathon Letters: One Family's Use of Support as They Took in, and Fell in Love with, a Troubled Child*, 2005.

Verny, Thomas, M.D. and Kelly, John, *The Secret Life of the Unborn Child*, Summit Books, New York, 1981, ISBN# 0-440-50565-8.

Weininger, Otto, Ph.D., *Time-In Parenting* (out of print).

Websites

www.aacps.org/infants/06annualreport.pdf

This website provides highlights of the federal and state law regulations governing early intervention services. Required services include: assistive devices and technology, audiology, evaluation, medical services (for evaluation/assessment), nursing, nutrition counseling, occupational therapy, psychological services, physical therapy, service coordination, social work, special instruction, speech/language therapy, and transportation.

www.aboutourkids.med.nyu.edu

An educational site primarily for parents focusing largely on child mental health. This website is the place to go when a doctor or therapist gives you a diagnosis that you don't know. They also have useful articles addressing many parenting issues.

www.acf.hhs.gov

This is part of the Administration For Children and Families, US Department of Health and Human Services. This site is helpful for obtaining information regarding Title IV-E regulations. It is great resource for federal policies regarding adoption. The site also includes the *Child Welfare Policy Manual,* which updates and reformats all of the existing relevant policy issuances (Policy Announcements and Policy Interpretation Questions) into an easy to use question-and-answer format.

www.adopt.org

This is the website of the National Adoption Center, which provides information about books, finances, how to adopt, race and culture, and articles from experts. A chat room and message board are also provided.

www.adopting.com

Adopting.com provides information and support regarding domestic and international adoption, as well as support for children with special needs. Online support groups are also provided.

www.adoption.about.com/parenting/adoption

Information is provided on TV programs and documentaries about foster care and adoption. Book reviews and scenarios about birth parents and grand parents are also included.

www.adopting.org

Adoption Profiles, LLC, provides adoption profiles, articles, resources (including respite care), and a chat room for those hoping to adopt, birthparents, adoptees, adoptive parents, adoption professionals, and foster parents.

www.adoptnet.org

The National Adoption Center's Learning Center offers a variety of online adoption chats, education, information, and support services. The Learning Center offers weekly moderated adoption chats, and the opportunity to interact with adoptive families and professionals through its message board.

www.attach.org

The Association for Treatment of Training in the Attachment of Children (ATTACh) website provides information about the latest research on attachment disorders. Their newsletter, available by subscription, is particularly informative. The organization also sponsors a yearly conference, which last year addressed everything from ethics to outcome research to helping parents to handle insurance, teachers and self-care.

www.attachmentparenting.org

Attachment Parenting International is an organization dedicated to educating and supporting parents in raising secure, joyful, and empathic children. They offer valuable resources for parent education, parent networking, and publications on attachment and related topics.

www.caseyfamilyservices.org

This website has a section devoted to post-adoption services and links to legislation regarding adoption subsidy. It also has a link to Casey Family Services available in different state localities.

www.childtrauma.org

This website of the Child Trauma Academy provides very valuable information for parents, mental health professionals and teachers on the effects of child trauma, and recommendations for supportive interventions.

www.childwelfare.gov

A service of the Children's Bureau, Administration for Children and Families, U.S. Department of Health and Human Services, this website provides resources to help prospective adoptive parents. It gives information regarding the costs involved in adoption, including information about grants, loans, employer benefits, tax credits, and subsidies.

www.davethomasfoundation.org

The Dave Thomas Foundation for Adoption website provides resources for individuals and organizations throughout the United States and Canada. A recent post lists the best adoption friendly employers.

www.nacac.org

This website of the North American Council on Adoptable Children provides a wealth of information regarding adoption and adoption subsidy regulations in every state, along with a range of resources such as parent support, post-adoption support and training. There is a Public Policy link, which outlines new or pending legislation regarding adoption. It also provides links regarding tax credits for adopted children. The site contains links to NACAC representatives in each state who give guidance regarding federal and state adoption laws and regulations.

www.naic.acf.hhs.gov

National Adoption Information Clearinghouse. This website provides lists of resources for families, both birth and adoptive, including statistics, legal and other information, support services, and information about birth parent searches.

www.nami.org

The National Alliance on Mental Illness (formerly National Alliance for the Mentally Ill) is the nation's largest grassroots health organization dedicated to improving the lives of persons living with serious mental illness and their families. Their website provides support, education, advocacy, and research.

www.nimh.nih.gov

The National Institute of Mental Health is the largest scientific organization in the world dedicated to research focused on the understanding, treatment, and prevention of mental disorders and the promotion of mental health.

www.wrightslaw.com

Parents, educators, advocates, and attorneys come to this website for accurate, reliable information about special education law and advocacy for children with disabilities. There are thousands of articles, cases, and resources.

www.zerotothree.org

Zero to Three provides a center for training services, a policy center, and resources for parents and professionals. Its annual conference provides professional development and training for experienced multidisciplinary child care, mental health, early intervention, and child welfare professionals.

APPENDIX D

ATTACh Accepted Definitions

Attachment

Attachment is a reciprocal process by which an emotional connection develops between an infant and his/her primary caregiver. It influences the child's physical, neurological, cognitive and psychological development. It becomes the basis for development of basic trust or mistrust, and shapes how the child will relate to the world, learn, and form relationships throughout life.

Attachment Therapist

The attachment therapist will:

- Promote and enhance a healthy reciprocal attachment between the child and the primary caregiver(s).
- Be well-trained in sound attachment and bonding theory and principles, and in child development.
- Primarily focus therapy upon the attachment relationship, not on the child's symptoms. Therefore, the parent is an active participant in the therapy.

- Practice attachment and bonding interventions that meet ATTACh's safety standards.
- Continue to develop skills through education specific to attachment.
- Use supervision and professional consultation for personal support.
- Support the appropriate authority and values of the parents.
- Provide attachment-focused skills development for parents.
- Take an active and directive stance in working with the child and family on core issues that they may find difficult to address.
- Work closely with the many systems affecting the child's life, such as extended family, school personnel and other professionals.

Attachment Therapy

Attachment therapy denotes the focus of the therapeutic process rather than a specific intervention technique. Attachment therapy can be of benefit to a person who has experienced early trauma and disruption in primary attachment relationships. The most important goal is to enable the person to form secure, reciprocal relationships so that he or she can heal from the trauma and other psychological disorders such as anxiety and depression caused by, or made worse by, the disruption of early attachment.

There are two primary areas of focus in attachment therapy. The first is to build a secure emotional attachment between the child and caregiver (or in the case of an adult in therapy, building the attachment between the client and the therapist). It is crucial to begin with this focus, since a trusting attachment relationship affords the security essential to address these clinical issues. Once the person is able to make use of a trusting relationship to learn new information and skills, the focus then shifts to healing the psychological, emotional, and behavioral issues that develop as a result of the parent-child disruption and/or early trauma. These clinical issues may include Posttraumatic Stress Disorder, grief and loss, depression, anxiety, and neuropsychological disorders. Attachment therapy can encompass and integrate a variety of treatment interventions. It is based on treatment theories drawn from an array of relevant therapeutic approaches including behavioral, cognitive, and psychodynamic. Attachment therapy can be used with cases which range from simple to complex. As in other therapies, complex cases are often best supported by an integrated team approach.

Disorders of Attachment

A disorder of attachment is a treatable condition in which there is a significant dysfunction in an individual's ability to trust or engage in reciprocal loving, lasting relationships. Disorders of attachment occur due to traumatic disruption or other interferences with the caregiver-child bond during the first years of life. It can distort future stages of development and impact a person's cognitive, neurological, social and emotional functioning. It may also increase risk of other serious emotional and behavioral problems. Note: for a medical definition of Reactive Attachment Disorder of Infancy or Early Childhood, 313.89, see the Diagnostic and Statistical Manual of Mental Disorders, IV-TR.

Dissociative Disorders

Dissociative disorders all feature a sudden, temporary alteration or dysfunction of memory, consciousness, identity, and behavior. Dissociative states refer to the "splitting off" from conscious awareness of some ordinarily familiar information, emotion, or mental function.

Evergreen

Evergreen is a city in Colorado which has been the North American center for a wide variety of models of attachment work since the late 1960's. It is erroneously referred to as a synonym for all attachment-based therapy.

Holding

Although the term "holding therapy" has been used in the past, holding is currently recognized as a technique which can be one part of a more comprehensive treatment for attachment issues during which other supportive therapeutic techniques may be utilized. Essential components include eye contact, appropriate touch, empathy, genuine expression of emotion, nurturance, reciprocity, safety and acceptance. While a variety of holding positions can be used, the physical safety of the client is the primary consideration.

Rage Reduction

Currently the term "rage reduction" refers to a therapeutic goal, not a specific technique. Reducing the client's rage in order to facilitate more adaptive emotional regulation, cognitive processing and relational capacity may be a goal of attachment therapy. In the early years of attachment work, the phrase referred to a confrontational and physically intrusive technique developed by Robert Zaslow, which was utilized to elicit rage in order to reduce resistance and thereby facilitate the healing of the child.

Rebirthing

Rebirthing is the name of an intervention which has been mistakenly identified with holding therapy. The term actually refers to a variety of processes designed to help people resolve trauma from around the time of birth.

Restraint

Restraint is the application of a physical, mechanical or chemical force on a person's body for the purpose of restricting the free movement of a person's body. Restraint is a safety intervention. Restraint is indicated and permitted as an emergency safety intervention for the protection of the person and/or others and/or property. Restraint is an intervention of last resort; it is not a therapeutic intervention.

Manual Restraint—A physical hands-on technique that restricts the movement or function of a person's body or portion of their body. The following are not considered restraint: holding a person without undue force to calm or comfort; holding a person's hand to safely escort them from one area to another; prompting or guiding a person who does not resist to assist in the activities of daily living.

Mechanical restraint—The use of a physical device to restrict the movement of a person or the movement or normal function of a portion of his or her body.

Chemical restraint—The administration of medication for the purpose of restraint.

Seclusion—Physically confining an individual alone in a room or limited space from which they are prohibited from leaving.

Standards for safe restraint

- Restraint is never used as punishment.
- Restraint is only practiced by those who have been specially trained in safe restraint techniques.
- Restraint should never interfere with a person's ability to breathe.
- As early as feasible in the restraint process, staff should inform the person of the behavioral criteria required for the restraint to be discontinued.
- Restraint should be discontinued when the individual meets the behavioral criteria.
- Restrained persons should be monitored continuously for physical safety.
- Due to the high risk associated with restraint, institutional settings such as hospitals require examination by a licensed doctor or registered nurse or physician's assistant, within one hour of the restraint, whenever a restraint is maintained over 20 minutes. This precaution may not be available in an outpatient setting. However, if the client is still out of control, combative and dangerous 20 minutes into the restraint, back-up medical assistance may need to be called to insure the client's safety.

Therapeutic Window

This is a concept about how to manage the emotional dimensions of trauma memories. The basic idea is that for treatment to be effective, there must be some emotion present (above the "sill" of the window), but not so much that the person becomes dysregulated (dissociated, uncommunicative, unable to engage), placing the person above the top of the window. Exposure to traumatic memories in small doses enables the person to

- manage the emotions
- develop skill at managing the traumatic memories and conditioned emotional responses
- develop confidence that he can manage the emotions associated with the trauma without become overwhelmed, which would strengthen, not lessen, the conditioned emotional response.

"The therapeutic window refers to a psychological midpoint between adequate and overwhelming activation of trauma-related emotions during treatment." (Briere, J., & Scott, C., (2006) Principles of Trauma Therapy, NY:Sage, pg. 125).

White Paper

A white paper typically argues a specific position or solution to a problem. The ATTACh *White paper on Coercion* was written regarding coercion in parenting and therapy, and presents research and arguments against the use of coercion.